MW01153389

Marty Soper

| Skill Area: | Study Skills |
| Interest Level: | Ages 12 thru Adult |

LinguiSystems®

3100 4th Avenue
East Moline, IL 61244

1-800-PRO IDEA
1-800-776-4332

Printed in the U.S.A.
ISBN 1-55999-256-5

ABOUT THE AUTHOR

Marty Soper

Marty Soper has been a school psychologist for 21 years. He is on the Special Education staff of the Northern Trails Area Education Agency. Professionally, Marty has a special interest in learning styles and parent training. Marty also teaches undergraduate courses in Psychology and Human Growth for the North Iowa Area Community College.

A trained puppeteer, Marty performs with the Kids on the Block program. He and his wife, Cindy, live in Hampton, Iowa and have two grown children. Marty enjoys home computing and collecting antique pins and badges.

DEDICATION

To Harold T. Webb, a special educator. Not only did you tell me what to do, but you showed me how to do it. Thanks — Marty

ACKNOWLEDGEMENTS

Thank you Cindy. Once again you knew the importance of time and space.

Thank you Molly Lyle and Lauri Vair. You and your team made me look good.

TABLE OF CONTENTS

SKILL CHART

Unit 1: Setting Goals	• critical thinking • setting goals • using time wisely	• sequencing • planning daily activities • assessing skills and interests
Unit 2: Managing Time	• understanding time concepts • prioritizing activities • using time wisely	• estimating time • using a calendar
Unit 3: Listening	• asking questions • following directions • interpreting verbal/nonverbal signals	• distinguishing fact from feeling • paraphrasing • expressing opinions
Unit 4: Taking Notes	• outlining • using graphic organizers • using shorthand • recognizing verbal signals • asking and answering questions • recognizing main ideas and supporting details	
Unit 5: Studying	• paying attention • problem solving • answering *Wh-* & *How* questions • using time wisely	• setting goals • paraphrasing • reading a textbook • preparing to study
Unit 6: Taking Tests	• planning • predicting • using resources • asking questions • following directions • understanding test questions • distinguishing between fact and opinion	
Unit 7: Learning Attitude	• asking questions • taking responsibility for actions • asking for help • handling stress	• problem solving • developing a positive attitude • understanding motivation
Unit 8: Learning Style	• understanding different learning styles (auditory, visual, tactile/kinesthetic) • identifying individual learning styles • strengthening auditory, visual, and tactile/kinesthetic skills • recognizing teaching styles • adapting learning styles to teaching styles	

INTRODUCTION

"I know he could do better if he'd just remember to do his homework."

"If she'd only pay attention in class, her grades would be much higher."

"I can give them a lot of extra help, but they have to want to learn."

He *could* do better.   She *does* need to learn how to pay attention.   They *do* have to want to learn.

But how do you help them, you ask?   *Crash Course for Study Skills* provides you with the how-to techniques for teaching your students the study skills they need for school success.

The "host" of *Crash Course for Study Skills* is 19-year-old Clinton D. Fentonbenton, a former student, who succeeded in school when he decided to learn better study skills.

Throughout *Crash Course for Study Skills*, Clinton provides an example of the success a student can experience in school when he takes responsibility for his own learning.   Clinton's observations, his opinions, and his up-beat humor keep the learning lively and meaningful.

In *Crash Course for Study Skills*, your students learn essential study skills through these eight units:

✔ Setting Goals   ✔ Studying

✔ Managing Time   ✔ Taking Tests

✔ Listening   ✔ Learning Attitude

✔ Taking Notes   ✔ Learning Style

Each unit of *Crash Course for Study Skills* helps your students assess and improve their individual study skills.   Designed to be used individually, in small groups, or with a class, each unit includes:

● an introduction of the skills taught in the unit

● a survey or rating scale to help your students assess their individual study-skill needs

● handouts, activities, and worksheets to teach and practice specific study skills

● *Amazing Facts*, or humorous tidbits, to keep learning fun

In addition to specific study skills like outlining, summarizing, and paraphrasing, your students will learn about study tools, like mnemonic devices, assignment books, and graphic organizers.

The variety of activities in each unit also promotes learning through three learning styles — auditory, visual, and tactile/kinesthetic — so your students can truly be successful.

Because each unit can be used independently of other units, you can pick the crash course that best suits your students' individual needs.

Wherever you start in *Crash Course for Study Skills*, don't forget to first introduce your students to Clinton in the *Hello* section on page 6.   You won't want your students to miss a minute as they join Clinton on the road to school success!

Hello

Hi! I'm Clinton D. Fentonbenton and I'm going to be your host for *Crash Course for Study Skills*. Before you ask, the *D* stands for Denton. That's right, my full name is Clinton Denton Fentonbenton.

Yeah, I know. But, it's *me.* I like the sound of Clinton Denton Fentonbenton.

Well, enough about my name. I want to say something about *Crash Course for Study Skills*. I think you'll find that the ideas in this book really work. And if you practice these ideas, studying will be easier and your grades will be higher.

"Why was I asked to host this book?" you might ask. First of all, everyone likes my name! Second, I was a student myself not long ago. I guess they figured I could help other students understand what studying is all about.

Third, I was once a very poor student. I mean, there for a while, my grades were really pathetic. I'm talking flunk-out city!

It wasn't until I had Mr. Justin for ninth grade English that my grades got better. Mr. Justin taught me that I had the power to make better grades — and that I could turn on that power simply by improving my study skills.

It sounds like I'm giving you a commercial about this book, doesn't it? Well, maybe I am . . . a little. Hey, everyone knows that you don't get good grades or bigger muscles or a better job without working. This book is only a tool. It's a tool you can use to build up your study skills. But remember, it's only a tool — YOU have to do the work.

Well, maybe I should quit talking now so you can get down to some serious work. But before I go, let's remember what my grandfather Clipton Fentonbenton always said — "Being successful is like eating a walnut. Before you can get to the good part, you gotta get cracking." Grandfather was always a little strange, but he was right. Let's "get cracking!"

You know, being a student is a lot like being a house builder. You have to follow some kind of plan to know what you are doing. If you don't have a plan to follow, you may never get what you want. You also might end up with a very strange looking house!

Are you good at planning? Well, I wasn't until I learned some easy tips for doing it. Now, I'll pass those tips along to you.

In this unit, you will learn how to plan so you can accomplish what's important to you. You'll learn how to use a To-Do list to plan what you do each day.

You'll also learn the difference between short-range goals and long-range goals. Then, you'll practice setting goals for:

- ✔ your study time
- ✔ your free time
- ✔ your career
- ✔ your life in general!

If you can plan and set goals, you can be successful at anything you do!

Self-Rating Scale

How well do you set goals and make plans?
Complete *Clinton D. Fentonbenton's Goal-Setting Rating Scale* to find out.   It's important that you answer the questions honestly.   (Honestly!)

After each statement below, circle A, B, C, or D.

Clinton D. Fentonbenton's Goal-Setting Rating Scale

almost always A	most of the time B	sometimes C	almost never D			
1. I think it's important to plan.			A	B	C	D
2. I plan what I'll do each day.			A	B	C	D
3. I make lists of things to do.			A	B	C	D
4. I plan how I'll use my free time.			A	B	C	D
5. I use an assignment sheet or assignment notebook.			A	B	C	D
6. I plan my writing assignments before I begin to write.			A	B	C	D
7. I get my studying "out of the way" so I can enjoy the rest of my day or evening.			A	B	C	D
8. Before I begin to study, I decide on certain goals to reach.			A	B	C	D
9. I begin studying for a test several days ahead of time.			A	B	C	D
10. I think about my future career.			A	B	C	D

Now, turn the page and see how you rate!

Self-Rating Scale, *continued*

Find your total points by using the guidelines below.

Give yourself 4 points for each A you circled.   _____ X 4 = _____

Give yourself 3 points for each B you circled.   _____ X 3 = _____

Give yourself 2 points for each C you circled.   _____ X 2 = _____

Give yourself 1 point for each D you circled.   _____ X 1 = _____

Total Points   = _____

Check the rating below that matches your total points.

☐ 10 – 15 points   **GULP!**   I need to improve my goal-setting skills.

☐ 16 – 23 points   **YIKES!**   I'm getting better, but I still need to improve my goal-setting skills.

☐ 24 – 31 points   **WOW!**   I have good goal-setting skills.

☐ 32 – 40 points   **BONUS!**   I have excellent goal-setting skills.

Don't Forget

Unless you're a genius or something, you probably forget to do things sometimes. That's why some people write notes to themselves or make lists.

Personally I, Clinton D. Fentonbenton, am a list maker. I make grocery lists, things-to-do lists, people-to-see lists, and supply lists. Sometimes, I make lists just for fun!

I went to a movie last night. It was so boring I sat there in the dark and made a list of the top three most boring movies of all time. So here it is. Clinton D. Fentonbenton's Top Three Most Boring Movies of All Time! (Drumroll, please.)

The Wonderful World of Oatmeal

The Texas Papercut Massacre

Fluffy: Space Dog From Heck

How would you fill in the following lists?

Four Favorite TV Shows of All Time

1. _____   3. _____

2. _____   4. _____

Two Most Boring Sports

1. _____   2. _____

Four Toppings Needed for Pizza Supremo!

1. _____   3. _____

2. _____   4. _____

To-Do Lists

Oh sure, making lists can be fun. But mostly I use lists to help me remember things.

If I have to do something special, like get a haircut, I'll write myself a little note. I put the note in my shirt pocket to remind me to get a haircut. When I get my haircut, I tear up the note. If I don't get my haircut, then I carry the note until I remember to do it. It really works!

If I have a lot of things to do, I make a list of them. Then, as I do each one, I get that great feeling of accomplishment by checking that item off my list.

To-Do List

☑ Read story in English book.
☑ Feed pet skunk. (carefully!)
☐ Clean garage.
☐ Take brother to the mall.
☐ Help Mrs. Stalecracker with rosebushes.

Here's my To-Do list for today.

Write your To-Do list for today below. As you do each thing on your list, check it off.

☐ 1. _____

☐ 2. _____

☐ 3. _____

☐ 4. _____

☐ 5. _____

☐ 6. _____

☐ 7. _____

☐ 8. _____

☐ 9. _____

☐ 10. _____

More To Do

Use the To-Do list below to plan your day.   List the ordinary things you'll do (homework), and the extraordinary (take my girlfriend, Wendy, to the movies).

Keep this list with you and check off each thing as you do it.   Then, save this list to use with the next worksheet.

	TO-DO LIST
☐	1.
☐	2.
☐	3.
☐	4.
☐	5.
☐	6.
☐	7.
☐	8.
☐	9.
☐	10.

Change Is Good

If I can't get everything done on my To-Do list, then I pick just a few things to do. Sometimes I even need to *revise*, or change, my list because what I thought was important on Monday isn't as important on Tuesday.

Go back to the *More To Do* worksheet on page 12. Did you do everything on your list? Revise your list for today and rewrite it below. Add new things to your list, too, if you need to. Remember to check things off as you do them.

TO-DO LIST	
☐	1.
☐	2.
☐	3.
☐	4.
☐	5.
☐	6.
☐	7.
☐	8.
☐	9.
☐	10.

Taking Aim

You can plan what you do by setting goals. A *goal* is something you plan to do. Any goal you want to reach quickly is called a *short-range goal*. A short-range goal is a goal you want to reach today, this week, or sometime this month.

Here are some examples of Lucy Wallhanger's short-range goals and when she plans to reach them.

Short-range Goal: *I will finish my history assignment.*

When: *today*

Short-range Goal: *I will put $25 in my savings account.*

When: *this month*

List three of your short-range goals below. After each goal, tell when you plan to reach it.

1. Short-range Goal: _____

_____

When: _____

2. Short-range Goal: _____

_____

When: _____

3. Short-range Goal: _____

_____

When: _____

Step By Step

Here is another example of a short-range goal.   To reach a short-range goal, you may have to take several steps.

Notice the steps Dan will take to reach his short-range goal.

Short-range Goal: *I will pass basketball tryouts in two weeks.*

What steps will Dan take to reach his goal?

Practice shooting.

Lift weights.

Play basketball with my friends.

Run every other day.

Ask the basketball coach for advice.

List two of your short-range goals below and the steps you'll take to reach them.   Remember, short-range goals are goals you want to reach today, this week, or sometime this month.

1.   Short-range Goal: _____

What steps will I take to reach my goal?

_____

_____

_____

_____

2.   Short-range Goal: _____

What steps will I take to reach my goal?

_____

_____

_____

_____

Study Time

You can set short-range goals for your study time, too. Plan your study-time goals by following these tips:

✔ Decide which subject you will study first, second, third, and so on.

✔ Decide how long you will study before you take a break.

✔ Decide how long your breaks will be. (Please note: a break is shorter than the actual study time!)

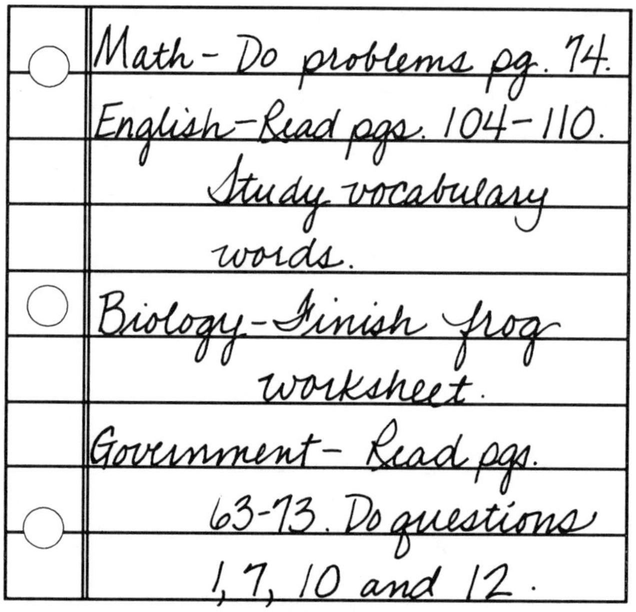

Math – Do problems pg. 74.
English – Read pgs. 104-110. Study vocabulary words.
Biology – Finish frog worksheet.
Government – Read pgs. 63-73. Do questions 1, 7, 10 and 12.

Here's a peek at Sandy Stickgum's assignment notebook.

Help Sandy Stickgum complete her study goals by filling in the chart below.

Order	Subject	Length of Study Period	Length of Break
1			
2			
3			
4			
5			

Your Study Goals

Fill in the chart below with short-range goals for your study time.   Use your real assignments.
Remember to follow these tips for planning your study time:

✔ Decide which subject you will study
   first, second, third, and so on.

✔ Decide how long you will study before
   you take a break.

✔ Decide how long your breaks will be.

Order	Subject	Length of Study Period	Length of Break
1			
2			
3			
4			
5			

Free Time

To make the most of your *free time*, or your time away from school, you can set goals, too. You can decide what you'll do with friends, what sports or hobbies you'll do, or what other responsibilities you'll take care of during your free time.

What are your free-time goals for today? Fill in the chart below with the following information:

- ✔ what you'll do as a free-time activity
- ✔ when you'll do each free-time activity

As you do each activity, check it off your list.

Check	Free-Time Activity	When
☐		
☐		
☐		
☐		
☐		
☐		
☐		

Short-Range Planning

As you can see, it's important to set short-range goals for many things.   To be a good planner, you need to practice setting goals often and try to reach them.

Use the chart below to set short-range goals for yourself for today, this week, or sometime this month. Describe each goal and when you'd like to reach it.   Remember to check off each goal when you reach it!

Check	Goal	When
☐		
☐		
☐		
☐		
☐		
☐		
☐		
☐		

Long-Range Goals

Do you have a goal that might take you a long time to reach?   Any goal you want to reach in several months or years is called a *long-range goal*.   For example, you might have a long-range goal of graduating from high school or playing in a band.

What long-range goals do you have?   List your long-range goals below and decide when you plan to reach them.

1.   Long-range Goal: _____

     When: _____

2.   Long-range Goal: _____

     When: _____

3.   Long-range Goal: _____

     When: _____

Ladder to Success

Working on a long-range goal is like climbing a ladder.   Each smaller goal is a step up that ladder. Once you climb all the steps, you're at the top of the ladder.   You have reached your long-range goal.

Here's an example of Maria's long-range goal. Maria is a 17-year-old junior.   She wants to become a professional photographer.   To reach that long-range goal, she must first reach several other goals.

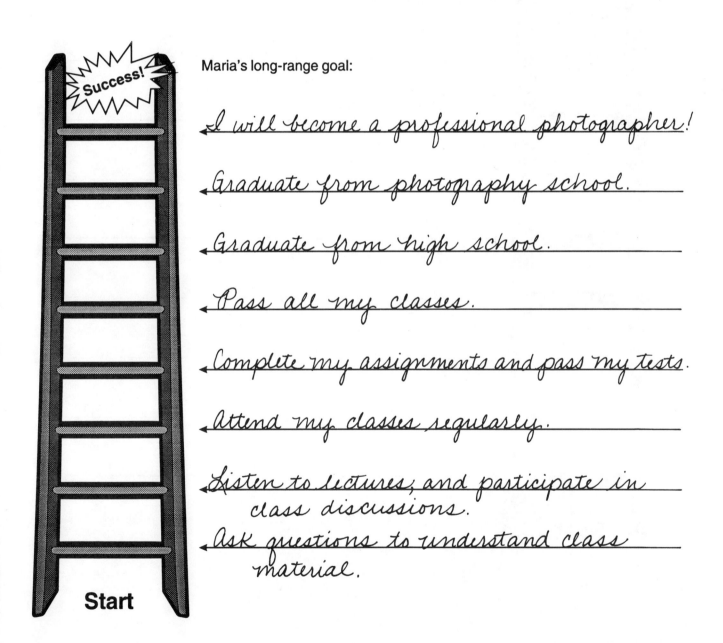

Maria's long-range goal:

I will become a professional photographer!

Graduate from photography school.

Graduate from high school.

Pass all my classes.

Complete my assignments and pass my tests.

Attend my classes regularly.

Listen to lectures, and participate in class discussions.

Ask questions to understand class material.

Step Up to Success

Meet Andy Cash.   Andy is a freshman this year.   He enjoys being with his friends and listening to music.   Andy's long-range goal is to have his own stereo system.

Fill in the steps of Andy's *Ladder to Success*.   Remember, it might take Andy several months or years to reach his long-range goal.

Andy's long-range goal:

I'll own a stereo system.

Long-Range Planning

What are your long-range goals? Use the ladder below to plan how you'll reach one of your long-range goals. Remember, it may take you several months or years to follow all the steps to your goal. Climb that ladder to success!

Success!

Start

My long-range goal:

Making Plans

Practice your goal-setting skills! Here's a situation that calls for a plan. It's up to you to decide what your goal is and how you can reach it.

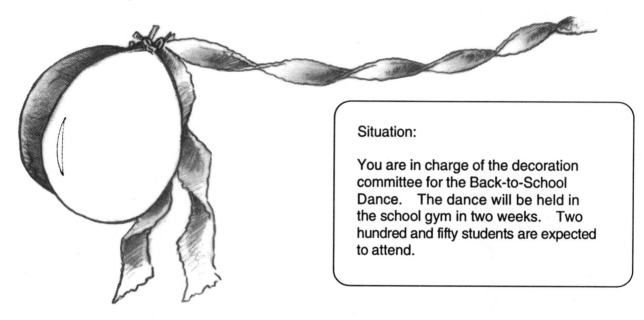

Situation:

You are in charge of the decoration committee for the Back-to-School Dance. The dance will be held in the school gym in two weeks. Two hundred and fifty students are expected to attend.

1. What is your goal? _____

_____

2. List the steps you'll take to reach your goal.

_____

_____

_____

_____

_____

_____

3. Is this a short-range goal or a long-range goal? Why? _____

_____

More Planning

Here's another situation that needs your immediate attention!   You must decide what your goal will be.   You must also plan how to best reach your goal.

> Situation:
>
> Your social studies teacher, Mrs. Armknuckle, has just given you an assignment.   You are to write a paper on the history of your community. Your paper must be at least four pages long.   It is due one week from today.

1. What is your goal? _____

    _____

2. List the steps you'll take to reach your goal.

    _____

    _____

    _____

    _____

    _____

    _____

3. Is this a short-range goal or a long-range goal?   Why? _____

    _____

Your Turn!

Create a situation for someone else to practice goal setting.   Write the situation in the space below.

Then, give your paper to someone else.   Have that person answer the questions below.   Compare ideas when you're done!

Situation:

_____

_____

_____

_____

_____

1. What is your goal? _____

_____

2. List the steps you'll take to reach your goal.

_____

_____

_____

_____

_____

_____

3. Is this a short-range goal or a long-range goal?   Why? _____

_____

Career Goals

You can also set a long-range goal for your future called a *career goal*.   A career goal is what you plan to do after you graduate from high school.

What should you think about when you choose a career goal?   Read each statement below.   Check *Yes* if it describes something important to think about.   Check *No* if you don't think it's important.

Yes   No

☐   ☐   1.   I think I should have a career goal.

☐   ☐   2.   It's okay to change my career goal.

☐   ☐   3.   I can enjoy working.

☐   ☐   4.   I should choose a career goal based on my interests.

☐   ☐   5.   I should choose a career goal based on my skills.

☐   ☐   6.   I should choose a career goal based on how much money I can make.

☐   ☐   7.   I should choose a career goal because someone else thinks it would be right for me.

Clinton's Career

My family tells me that when I was five, I wanted to be a fire truck.   When I was ten, I was going to be a professional wrestler.   Can you see me as *Mad Dog Fentonbenton*, the world's meanest wrestler? Right, neither could I!

At age fourteen, I thought I wanted to be a doctor. But then I found out how long doctors have to go to school.

See how my career goals have changed over the years?   I think that's pretty normal.   Most people change their minds several times before they decide on the best career for themselves.

A few years ago, I started thinking about my future and what long-range goals I wanted to accomplish. Then, I developed a plan that would lead me to my career goal.   Right now, I'm taking steps to be a travel agent.   Can't you just see it . . . *Clinton D. Fentonbenton's Travel Agency*?   I get excited just thinking about it!

What career goals have you thought about?   Fill in the information below.

When I was five, I wanted to be a _____.

When I was ten, I wanted to be a _____.

Now I want to be a _____.

Interests and Skills

When you plan your career goal, you need to think about your *interests*, or the things you like to do. You also need to think about your *skills*, or the things you do well.

What are your interests and skills?   Complete *Clinton D. Fentonbenton's Career Interest Survey* to find out!   Circle the answer that best describes you.

Clinton D. Fentonbenton's Career Interest Survey

1. I like to work mostly (inside   outside).

2. I like to work mostly (with people   by myself).

3. I like to work mostly (using my hands   using my head).

4. School is (easy for me   okay for me   difficult for me).

5. I would like to live in a (large community   medium-sized community   small community).

6. What are three interests I have?   Interests are the things I like to do.

   a. _____

   b. _____

   c. _____

7. What are three skills I have?   Skills are the things I do well.

   a. _____

   b. _____

   c. _____

Now, look at your answers.   What are three career goals that might fit your interests and skills?   Talk to a parent, a guidance counselor, a friend, or a classmate for ideas, too.

1. _____

2. _____

3. _____

Career Choices

If you had to choose a career goal right this minute, what would it be?   Plan how you'll reach your career goal by using the ladder below.   Remember, it may take several steps to reach your goal.

Success!

My career goal:

← _____

← _____

← _____

← _____

← _____

← _____

← _____

Start

Now, share your career goal with your class by doing one of the following activities.   Use the back of this page to write notes about how you plan to share your career goal.

☐ Read about your career in the library.   Then, give a short oral report to share what you learn.

☐ Write a report explaining why you think your career goal would be good for you.

☐ Make a model or a collage that helps explain your career goal.

☐ Interview someone who has the career you've chosen.   Report how this person reached this goal.   Tell what things you would do the same or differently.

☐ Create an idea of your own to share your career goal.

Practice Is Important

It's time to practice what you've learned!   Choose some activities you could do to practice planning and goal setting.   Use the list below to help you.

☐ Keep a To-Do list every day for one week.   Revise or change your list when you need to.

☐ Choose two short-range goals for one week and try to reach them.

☐ Ask a parent or other adult to describe a short-range goal.

☐ Make a study plan and follow it for a week.

☐ Explain what a long-range goal is to someone younger than you.

☐ Choose a long-range goal to reach in the next year.   Then, have a friend or family member help you reach it.

☐ Ask your guidance counselor for information about your career goal.

☐ Develop your career goals and personal goals for five years from now.

☐ Join a club at school or in your community.   Get on its planning committee.

Now, write down the activities you try in the chart below.   Fill in the following information for each activity:

- ✔ Tell when you did the activity.
- ✔ Describe the activity.
- ✔ Explain how well you think the activity worked.

Date	Activity	How Well It Worked
September 6	Made a weekly study plan for English.	Helped me get a B on my vocabulary quiz!

Clinton D. Fentonbenton's **Amazing Facts**

Amazing Fact #1: The most organized person in the world is Mr. Maxwell Q. Tipp of Springfield, Missouri.   Mr. Tipp is so well organized that he keeps his sock drawer in alphabetical order!

Amazing Fact #2: The least organized person in the world is Ms. Sherly U.R. Kidding of Hampton, Iowa.   On August 8, 1973, Ms. Kidding attempted to organize a trip to her kitchen and was unsuccessful.

Amazing Fact #3: Rose Thornbush needs help planning her social calendar.   Last week there was a really great party at Jerry's house, but Rose didn't go.   The invitation said from 8 to 12, and Rose is 16!

If you ask any successful person in the work world about success, he will tell you that part of becoming successful is being at the right place at the right time.

In this unit, you'll learn how to manage your time wisely so you can become successful. You'll practice things like:

✔ keeping a time log

✔ estimating the time it takes to do something

✔ prioritizing your activities

✔ using a weekly or monthly calendar

No one can remember all his appointments all the time without some help. Until my Uncle Quinton Fentonbenton started using a weekly calendar, he was always at the wrong place at the wrong time. In fact, he almost got fired from his job because of this problem. You see, he's a bus driver!

Time-Management Rating Scale

Time out! How well do you manage your time? Complete *Clinton D. Fentonbenton's Time-Management Rating Scale* to find out. Don't foul! Be sure to circle only the answers that are true for you.

After each statement, circle A, B, C, or D.

Clinton D. Fentonbenton's Time-Management Rating Scale

almost always A	most of the time B	sometimes C	almost never D			
1. I wear a watch.			A	B	C	D
2. I know what month and day it is.			A	B	C	D
3. I know the dates of holidays.			A	B	C	D
4. I can plan ahead and organize my time.			A	B	C	D
5. I hand in my assignments on time.			A	B	C	D
6. I use a calendar to keep track of my daily schedule, like times for dances, ball games, and tests.			A	B	C	D
7. I am on time for classes, meetings, and appointments.			A	B	C	D
8. I plan my daily activities from most important to least important.			A	B	C	D
9. I can estimate the time it will take me to do something.			A	B	C	D
10. I get my studying "out of the way" so I can enjoy the rest of my day or evening.			A	B	C	D

Now, turn the page and see how you rate!

Time-Management Rating Scale, *continued*

Find your total points by using the guidelines below.

Give yourself 4 points for each A you circled. ＿＿＿＿ X 4 = ＿＿＿＿

Give yourself 3 points for each B you circled. ＿＿＿＿ X 3 = ＿＿＿＿

Give yourself 2 points for each C you circled. ＿＿＿＿ X 2 = ＿＿＿＿

Give yourself 1 point for each D you circled. ＿＿＿＿ X 1 = ＿＿＿＿

Total Points = ＿＿＿＿

Check the rating below that matches your total points.

☐ 10 – 15 points **TECHNICAL FOUL!**   I need to improve my time-management skills.

☐ 16 – 23 points **DOUBLE DRIBBLE!**   I'm getting better, but I still need to improve my time-management skills.

☐ 24 – 31 points **SLAM DUNK!**   I have good time-management skills.

☐ 32 – 40 points **GAME WINNER!**   I have excellent time-management skills.

Watching Time

One important key to good *time management*, or handling your time, is being aware of time.

How aware of time are you?   Check the sentence below that best describes you.

- [ ] 1.   I am *always* aware of time.   I run like a $500 nuclear-powered combination blender/watch.

- [ ] 2.   I am *usually* aware of time.   I run like a $100 battery-powered combination toothpick/watch.

- [ ] 3.   I am *sometimes* aware of time.   I run like a $1000 submarine-powered combination periscope/watch sometimes, and a 2¢ went-through-the-washer watch other times.

- [ ] 4.   I am *seldom* aware of time.   I run like a $10 plastic Saturday-morning cartoon watch.

- [ ] 5.   I am *never* aware of time.   I run like a 97¢ egg timer with half the sand missing.

Use the space below to draw a watch that best describes you.

Why does your description fit you? _____

Does your description fit you all the time? _____

What kind of a watch would you like to be? _____

It's About Time

When it comes to time management, it's good to know the basics.   Use this page to review what you already know about time.   Just for fun, have a classmate time you.

1. There are _____ seconds in a minute.

2. There are _____ minutes in a half hour.

3. There are _____ minutes in an hour.

4. There are _____ hours in a day.

5. There are _____ days in a week.

6. There are _____ weeks in a year.

7. There are _____ months in a year.

8. There are _____ years in a decade.

9. I would look at a _____ to know what time it is.

10. I would look at a _____ to know what day it is.

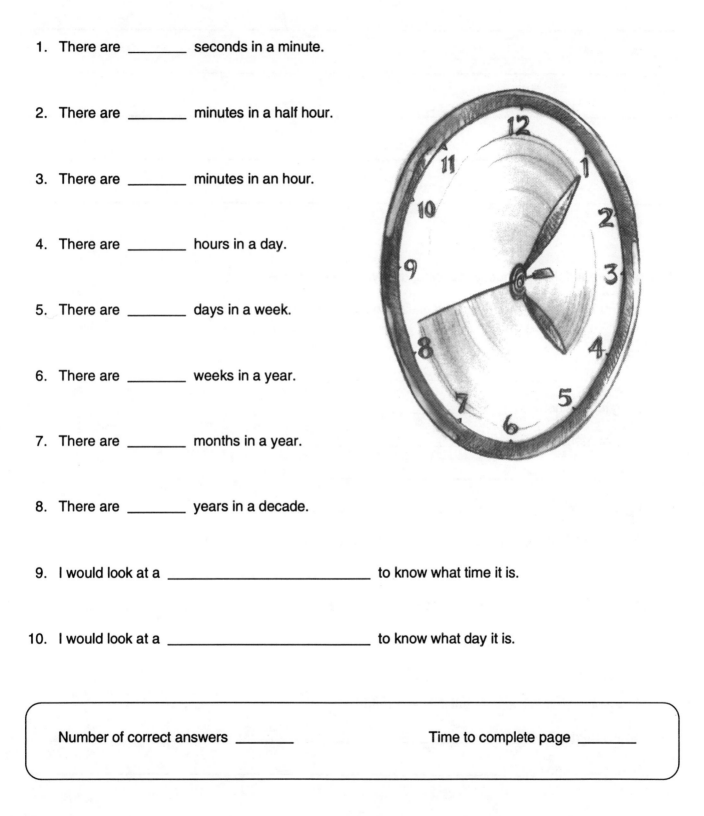

Number of correct answers _____   Time to complete page _____

Your Daily Schedule

How do you use your time?   Make a list of everything you do during a typical weekday.

_____   _____

_____   _____

_____   _____

_____   _____

_____   _____

Now, answer the following questions about how you use your time.

1.   How much time during a typical weekday do you spend:

at school?   _____

at your job?   _____

doing jobs at home?   _____

with your family?   _____

having fun?   _____

watching TV?   _____

sleeping and eating?   _____

2.   How do you spend most of your time?   _____

_____

3.   How would your list be different if it were made:

for a Saturday?   _____

three years ago?   _____

Keeping a Time Log

A *time log* is a list of times you do a specific activity each day.   Keeping a time log can help you become more aware of how you use your time.   Here's an example of Kate Clocktower's time log.

7:00 to 7:30	shower, breakfast	1:30 to 2:30	Global Studies
7:30 to 8:30	dress, go to school	2:30 to 3:30	Art
8:30 to 9:30	Biology	3:30 to 5:30	work
9:30 to 10:30	Math	5:30 to 6:00	free time
10:30 to 11:30	Gym/Vocal Music	6:00 to 6:30	supper
11:30 to 12:00	lunch	6:30 to 8:00	study
12:00 to 12:30	study hall	8:00 to 10:00	free time
12:30 to 1:30	English	10:00 to —	ready for bed

Use the time log below to write your daily activities.

to		to	
to		to	
to		to	
to		to	
to		to	
to		to	
to		to	
to		to	

Estimating Time

Do you know how much time it takes you to shower or to walk to each of your classes?   If you can *estimate*, or guess, how much time it takes to do an activity, you can plan your time more wisely.

Estimate how much time you need to do each activity below.   Later, time each activity with a watch so you know the exact amount of time it takes.

	Your Guess	**Exact Amount of Time**
1. brush your teeth	_____	_____
2. take a shower	_____	_____
3. get ready for school	_____	_____
4. get to school	_____	_____
5. walk from class to class	_____	_____
6. eat lunch	_____	_____
7. get to work	_____	_____
8. do tonight's homework	_____	_____
9. write your name 8 times	_____	_____

Now, try this activity.   Have a friend or your teacher use a watch with a second hand to time you.
Raise your hand when you think one minute has passed.   Try to estimate different times the same way.

Discuss the meaning of these sentences about time.

I just don't have enough time.

Time flies when you're having fun.

Don't waste time.

We shouted at the same time.

There's no time like the present.

Time is money.

Time is on my side.

Prioritize Your Time

Here's a list of things going on in my life today. I'm feeling a lot of pressure to do all of these things. But I know I probably can't do all of them! What should I do?

wash car
meet Lin Than for video games
clean my room
study for History exam
help clean the garage
take a nap
help youth group project at City Park
get hair cut
go to Aunt Fanny's retirement party

prioritize: to put in order of importance

Please help me prioritize my list using these guidelines. Write the activities I need to do in order of priority.

✔ **High Priority**   It's very important for me to do this activity today.

✔ **Low Priority**   I can do this activity another day.

High Priority   1. _____

2. _____

3. _____

4. _____

5. _____

6. _____

7. _____

8. _____

Low Priority   9. _____

High Priority

What do you need to do today?   Write your list of activities below.

1. _____

2. _____

3. _____

4. _____

5. _____

6. _____

7. _____

8. _____

9. _____

10. _____

Now, write your list of activities in order of priority.   Remember the guidelines below.

> ✔ **High Priority**   It's very important for me to do this activity today.
>
> ✔ **Low Priority**   I can do this activity another day.

High Priority

1. _____

2. _____

3. _____

4. _____

5. _____

6. _____

7. _____

8. _____

9. _____

Low Priority   10. _____

Now-24-Week-Month Plan

Here's a way to order your activities by time.   Try my *Now-24-Week-Month Plan*!

Now	Decide which activities you need to do right now.
24	Decide which activities you need to do in the next 24 hours.
Week	Decide which activities you need to do in the next week.
Month	Decide which activities you need to do in the next month.

So that's how it works.   Just ask yourself — *Now, 24, Week,* or *Month*? — and you'll know when to do the activity.

List six activities you need to do below.   Arrange your list so the first activity is your highest priority, and so on.   Then, write *Now, 24, Week,* or *Month* in front of each activity to tell when you need to do it.

When	Activity

Time-Management Tips

Here are nine tips that help me manage my time better.   Discuss these tips with someone else.   Talk about why each tip might help you manage your time better.   Then, explain your thinking on the line below the tip.

Tip 1:   *Have a plan.*   Know when to start and know when to finish.

_____

Tip 2:   *Write notes to yourself.*   Remind yourself what your plan is.

_____

Tip 3:   *Once you start a project, try to finish it.*

_____

Tip 4:   *Don't waste time.*   If you need help, ask for it.

_____

Tip 5:   *Be five minutes early to all appointments.*

_____

Tip 6:   *Make sure all your clocks and watches have the correct time.*

_____

Tip 7:   *Don't try to "make up time" by being unsafe (like speeding in a car, etc.).*

_____

Tip 8:   *Do difficult projects first.*   You'll be fresher and more alert.

_____

Tip 9:   *Prioritize your activities.*   Do the most important things first.

_____

Now, add a tip of your own.   Explain why it helps you manage your time better.

Tip 10: _____

_____

Calendar Quiz

A calendar is a great tool for managing time.   Complete *Clinton D. Fentonbenton's Calendar Quiz* to review what you know about calendars.

Clinton D. Fentonbenton's Calendar Quiz

List the twelve months of the year in order.   (No fair looking at a calendar unless you really have to!)

1.	7.
2.	8.
3.	9.
4.	10.
5.	11.
6.	12.

Think of eight holidays during the year.   Then, write the name and month of each holiday below.

	Holiday	Month
1.		
2.		
3.		
4.		
5.		
6.		
7.		
8.		

Monthly Calendar

Writing your activities on a *monthly calendar* can help you remember what you need to do. You can remind yourself that Mr. Watertrout is giving a biology test next Tuesday. Or you can remember not to sign up for work on Saturday the 20th because you're going to the Electric Earthworm's concert.

Here's what my monthly calendar for January looks like.

❄ ❄ ❄ ❄ *January* ❄ ❄ ❄ ❄						
Sunday	**Monday**	**Tuesday**	**Wednesday**	**Thursday**	**Friday**	**Saturday**
	1 *New Year's Day Football!*	2	3 *Work 4–9*	4	5 *Dentist Appointment 2:15*	6
7 *Family Reunion 1–5 pm*	8	9 *Biology Exam Chp 6–8*	10	11 *Student Senate Meeting 7:30 pm*	12	13 *Work 9–3*
14	15 *History Paper Due*	16	17 *Work 4–9*	18	19	20 *Earthworm Concert 8:00 pm*
21	22	23	24	25	26 *Jacquilie's Party*	27 *Work 9–3*
28	29	30	31 *Work 4–9*			

List activities you can remember by using a calendar. Think of all the activities you might have in a year.

1. _____
2. _____
3. _____
4. _____
5. _____
6. _____
7. _____

8. _____
9. _____
10. _____
11. _____
12. _____
13. _____
14. _____

Your Monthly Calendar

Use this monthly calendar to plan your activities.

_____ *(month)*						
Sunday	*Monday*	*Tuesday*	*Wednesday*	*Thursday*	*Friday*	*Saturday*

Weekly Calendar

Sometimes, I manage my time by using a *weekly calendar*. This kind of calendar shows only one week on a page. The weekly calendar gives you plenty of room to write your activities for each day. There is also a space to write notes on anything else you need to do that week. Here's a page from my past.

The Week of September 14 thru September 20

14 Monday *Math Quiz* *Haircut 4:00 pm*	**18** Friday *Football Game 7:30*
15 Tuesday	**19** Saturday *School Dance 8:00*
16 Wednesday *3:30 Art Club*	**20** Sunday
17 Thursday *Mom's Birthday* *6:30 Piano Lesson*	Notes:

---

1. What are the advantages of using a weekly calendar instead of a monthly calendar?

_____

_____

2. What are the disadvantages of using a weekly calendar instead of a monthly calendar?

_____

_____

3. Would you prefer to use a monthly calendar or a weekly calendar? Why?

_____

Your Weekly Calendar

Use this weekly calendar to plan your activities.

Weekly Calendar

The Week of _____	thru _____
_____ Monday	_____ Friday
_____ Tuesday	_____ Saturday
_____ Wednesday	_____ Sunday
_____ Thursday	Notes:

Good Ideas Quiz

Here are six good ideas for managing your time.

It's a good idea to:

✔ be on time for all your classes, meetings, or appointments

✔ hand in all your assignments on time

✔ get your homework done early so you can enjoy your free time later

✔ have specific goals for your study time and your free time

✔ spend some time studying every day

✔ plan ahead so you don't run out of time

Now, complete my *Good Ideas Quiz*.   Choose the correct word from the box and write it in the blank.

Clinton D. Fentonbenton's Good Ideas Quiz

monthly	study	prioritize
plan	great	every day
calendar	weekly	assignments
	appointments	

1. Some people like to use a _____ calendar to plan what they'll do each week.

2. Successful people _____ ahead.

3. A _____ can help you remember appointments.

4. A _____ calendar will help you make plans for the month.

5. A wise student will have _____ goals.

6. To be a successful student, you should study _____.

7. It's cool to be on time for _____.

8. Good students always complete _____ on time.

9. It helps to _____ your activities so you do the most important things first.

10. It feels _____ to get homework done early.

Time For Practice

It's time to practice what you've learned! Choose some activities you can do to practice managing your time. Use the list below to help you.

☐ Wear a watch.

☐ Use a weekly calendar to plan your activities.

☐ Use a monthly calendar to plan your activities.

☐ Make a goal to be five minutes early for all appointments.

☐ List your activities in order of importance.

☐ Try the *Now-24-Week-Month Plan* to prioritize your activities.

☐ Work first, play later.

☐ Schedule your activities using a time log.

Now, write down the activities you try in the chart below. Fill in the following information for each activity:

✔ Tell when you did the activity.

✔ Describe the activity.

✔ Explain how well you think the activity worked.

Date	Activity	How Well It Worked
January 21	Kept a weekly calendar	Really helped me remember things!

Clinton D. Fentonbenton's
Amazing Facts

Amazing Fact #1: The first calendar was made in 6000 B.C. by a caveman named Grunk. Because it was made of stone and was very heavy, the "year" could only be one week long.

Amazing Fact #2: The new battery-operated watches have really gotten strange. Clara Clock bought a new watch. It doesn't keep very good time, but it makes a great cup of coffee.

Amazing Fact #3: In 1947, Erma Terma invented the first gasoline-powered calendar. It would have worked, but one day in December it ran out of gas and Christmas was 24 hours late.

In this unit, you'll learn how to be a good listener. The good listener is everyone's friend. We like it when people hear and understand us. If you stop to think about it, you probably like your best friend because he or she is a good listener. When a friend has a problem, you listen so you can understand.

The same thing is true when you try to understand a lesson in school. The better you can listen, the easier it is to learn and understand.

If you follow *Clinton D. Fentonbenton's Tips for Good Listening*, you can be a good listener, too.

Tip 1: Get ready to listen.

Tip 2: Concentrate on listening.

Tip 3: Show that you're listening.

By the way, do you know why rabbits have such big ears? So they can hear carrots whispering! Ha! Let's get on to the important stuff!

Listening Survey

How well do you listen?   Complete *Clinton D. Fentonbenton's Listening Survey* to find out.   After each statement below, circle A, B, C, or D.

almost always A	most of the time B	sometimes C	almost never D			
1. I learn best by listening.			A	B	C	D
2. I can follow spoken directions.			A	B	C	D
3. I can remember what I hear.			A	B	C	D
4. I act like I'm listening when the speaker is talking.			A	B	C	D
5. I ask questions if I don't understand something.			A	B	C	D
6. I watch the speaker's movements and gestures.			A	B	C	D
7. I can tell what type of mood the speaker is in.			A	B	C	D
8. I look the speaker in the eye while I listen.			A	B	C	D
9. I think about other things while I listen.			A	B	C	D
10. I usually take notes while I listen in class.			A	B	C	D
11. I think about what the speaker is saying.			A	B	C	D
12. I can figure out the message of the speaker.			A	B	C	D
13. I can remember details.			A	B	C	D
14. I look elsewhere while I listen to the speaker.			A	B	C	D
15. I need help to become a better listener.			A	B	C	D

Look back at your answers.   Do you listen better some times than you do other times?   Do you listen better in some places than you do in other places?   Do you listen better at certain times of the day? If you have good listening skills sometimes, you can have good listening skills ALL the time.   Read on to find out how.

Ready to Listen

Here are three tips to become a better listener.   You'll learn more about these tips in the next few pages.

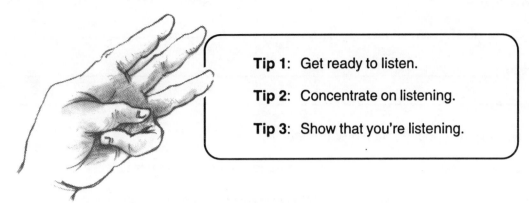

Tip 1: Get ready to listen.

Tip 2: Concentrate on listening.

Tip 3: Show that you're listening.

Let's talk about Tip 1 first.   Getting ready to listen to your teacher is important.   Here are some ways to get ready to listen:

✔ Tell yourself, "I'm ready to listen.   For the next 30 minutes I will try to understand what my teacher is talking about."

✔ If you're taking notes, have your paper, pen, and pencils out.

✔ If you're not taking notes, clear your desk.

✔ Sit up straight and lean forward in your chair.

✔ Make sure you can hear your teacher.

✔ Make sure you can see your teacher.

What other ways can you get ready to listen?

_____

_____

Concentration

Tip 2 for better listening is to concentrate on listening.   Look up the word *concentrate* in a dictionary. Write its definition below.

> **concentrate** _____

Here are some ways you can concentrate better on listening:

- ✔ Remind yourself where you are.   Don't let your mind wander to another place.

- ✔ Look for signals from the teacher that say, "This piece of information is important." Your teacher might point to some important information or tell you it will be on a test.

- ✔ Be willing to agree with what the teacher is saying.   If you're mentally arguing with the teacher, it's very difficult to listen and understand.

This is what Clara Ramjet is thinking about as she listens to her geometry teacher, Ms. Polly Gon.

What could Clara do to concentrate better in geometry class?

_____

_____

Sending Signals

When you concentrate on listening, it is important to pay attention to special signals the speaker may be sending you. *Signals* are clues that tell you what the speaker is saying is very important.

For example, if your geography teacher, Mrs. Oldbook, says, "The annual rainfall for the country of Kokotamia is less than 38 inches," and she writes *38* on the chalkboard at the same time, then this is a signal. This is a clue that a question about the annual rainfall of Kokotamia might be on your next geography test.

However, if Mrs. Oldbook usually writes EVERYTHING on the chalkboard, then this is not a good signal. Instead, you may find that Mrs. Oldbook signals important information by tapping her desk to make a particular point. Or maybe her voice gets a little louder or a little softer when she presents material that is important enough to be on a test.

Signals

✔ The teacher spells a new word.

✔ The teacher seems excited.

✔ The teacher uses gestures, like pointing to or underlining information.

✔ The teacher spends more time than usual on a topic.

✔ The teacher says something like, "This is important," or "Write this down," or "This will be on your next test."

What are some other signals your teachers use to tell you something is important?

_____

_____

On the Lookout

To be a good listener and a successful student, you must constantly look for signals from your teachers.   Signals will help you learn and remember important information.   Signals can be *verbal* or *nonverbal.*

Verbal Signals: signals given by using the voice

- ✔ *tone of voice*   Your teacher may use a more serious voice when the information is important to remember.

- ✔ *volume of voice*   Your teacher might talk louder or softer to get you to pay attention to what she's saying.

- ✔ *speed of speech*   Your teacher may talk slower to make sure you hear the important information.

- ✔ *repeating the information*   Your teacher may say the information more than once to make sure you hear it.

- ✔ *spending a long time on a topic*   Your teacher may take more time talking about information he thinks you should know.

Nonverbal Signals: signals given by using the body

- ✔ *eye contact*   Your teacher may look at you to make sure you are paying attention.

- ✔ *facial expression*   Your teacher might look more serious when he's explaining information you should remember.

- ✔ *gestures*   Your teacher may point to important information or tap a pencil when she's saying something important.

- ✔ *writing*   Your teacher may circle or underline information she thinks is important.

On the Lookout, *continued*

What verbal and nonverbal signals do your teachers use?   Fill in the chart below as you observe your teachers.

Teacher	Class	Verbal Signals	Nonverbal Signals

1, 2, 3

Now you're ready for Tip 3 for good listening.   To be a better listener, there are three tips you should follow.

Circle the correct answer below for **Tip 3**.

Tip 1:   Get ready to listen.

Tip 2:   Concentrate on listening.

Tip 3:   _____

    a.   Try not to put jelly beans in your ears.

    b.   Turn up the volume of your nuclear-powered Walkman.

    c.   Paint eyes on your eyelids so you can sleep in class.

    d.   Show that you are listening.

I hope you got the question above correct.   If you didn't, please visit with your teacher.

How do you show that you are listening?   I, Clinton D. Fentonbenton, have a few suggestions:

✔ *Get involved in the discussion.*   Give an opinion, express an idea, or give supporting information.

✔ *Show by your body language that you're listening.*   Sit up straight and lean forward slightly.

✔ *Make good eye contact.*   Look the speaker in the eye.

✔ *Ask questions when you don't understand.*

What other ways can you show that you're listening?

_____

_____

Any Questions?

One of the best ways to show that you're listening is to ask a question.   You might learn something, too!

Circle all the words below that ask a question.

who	the
is	this
went	when
these	those
there	where
what	see
came	how

Practice your question-asking skills by following these directions.

1. Write a question about football that asks *who.*

_____

2. Write a question about hamburgers that asks *when.*

_____

3. Write a question about your favorite music group that asks *where.*

_____

4. Write a question about space shuttles that asks *how.*

_____

Question, Please?

How do you feel about asking questions in class?   Check the answer that is right for you.   Then, discuss your answers with the rest of the class.

Yes   **No**

☐   ☐   Sometimes I feel foolish when I have to ask the teacher a question.

☐   ☐   Other students laugh or make fun of me when I say I don't understand something.

☐   ☐   Teachers usually get angry when I ask questions.

☐   ☐   I think students should ask questions when they need help.

Some students are afraid to ask teachers questions.   Some students think it will make them look foolish.   Other students think that if they ask a question, it will make the teacher angry.   Wrong-O! Most teachers are pleased when a student asks a question.

Asking questions lets the teacher know that you are listening, thinking, and trying to understand. Don't be afraid to ask your teacher to help you understand something.   You can say things like:

"Please tell me more about that."

"Let me see if I have this straight."

"Do you mean . . . ?"

"I'm not sure I understand."

"I don't think I got that.   Please say that again."

What do you say when you want to understand something better?

_____

_____

Question Asking

Practice asking questions in your classes. When you ask a question, fill in the chart below with information about the class, the teacher, and the question.

In the *Easy/Difficult* column, circle whether it was easy or difficult for you to ask the question.

Class	Teacher	Question	Easy/Difficult
Biology	Mr. Watertrout	Why don't frogs have gills?	(Easy) Difficult
			Easy Difficult
			Easy Difficult
			Easy Difficult
			Easy Difficult
			Easy Difficult
			Easy Difficult

Was it easy or difficult to ask questions? Why? _____

_____

With which teacher were you most comfortable asking questions? Why? _____

_____

Role Playing

Here's a quick reminder about how you can show good listening skills:

- ✔ *Get involved in the discussion.*   Give an opinion, express an idea, or give supporting information.

- ✔ *Show by your body language that you're listening.*   Sit up straight and lean forward slightly.

- ✔ *Make good eye contact.*   Look the speaker in the eye.

- ✔ *Ask questions when you don't understand.*

Now, practice identifying good listening skills or weak listening skills in a REAL situation.   With a partner, role-play the following situations.   One person is the teacher and the other is the student.

Situation 1:   The teacher teaches while the student shows weak listening skills.

Situation 2:   The teacher teaches while the student shows good listening skills.

Here are some topics you could teach:

how to add three-digit numbers   how to study for a test

how to find a word in the dictionary   why humans need plants and trees

Your own idea _____

After you role-play, list the things you noticed that showed good or weak listening skills.

Good Listening Skills	Weak Listening Skills
1. _____	1. _____
2. _____	2. _____
3. _____	3. _____
4. _____	4. _____
5. _____	5. _____

Following Directions

Following directions is very important, especially if you're a student. The directions you get in class are usually spoken. Spoken directions are also called *verbal directions*.

This page will help you learn how to follow verbal directions better. In the box below, give two examples of when you follow verbal, or spoken, directions during your day.

Example 1: _____

_____

Example 2: _____

_____

Here are five things you can do to follow verbal directions better:

1. *Get ready to listen.* Prepare your mind to receive information. Say to yourself, "Look out! This stuff is important."

2. *Make a mental picture.* In your mind, see yourself doing whatever the directions say you should do.

3. *Whisper the directions to yourself.* Repeat the directions several times in a low voice. This will make it easier for the information to "get into" your memory.

4. *Listen for key action words.* Pay close attention to words like *read*, *draw*, or *write* that tell you exactly what to do.

5. *Write the directions down.* Writing down directions will help you remember what you are to do.

Follow Me, Please

Practice following verbal directions.   With a partner, take turns reading the following lists of directions.

One student should read the directions while the other student follows the directions.   Have a pencil and paper ready.

List A

1.   Write the sentence *I like gum.*

2.   Circle the word *gum.*

List B

1.   Draw a small square in the center of the page.

2.   Draw a small triangle to the right of the square.

3.   Draw a wavy line from the square to the triangle.

List C

1.   Write your name in the upper left-hand corner of the page.

2.   Number your paper 1 through 10 on the left side of the page.

3.   Draw a square around number 7 and a circle around number 3.

4.   Write the words *good student* next to number 7.

List D

1.   Draw a triangle in the center of the page.

2.   Write the numbers 1 through 15 on the top of the page.

3.   Touch your left hand to your right ear twice.

4.   Draw lines from the triangle to the numbers 3 and 12.

Listen Up!

Listening is very important in the classroom. Listening is important when we talk to people, too. When we listen to other people, we pay attention to both the *facts* and the *feelings* in what they say.

We listen for the *facts* in a message so we remember the information we hear.

> **Facts**
>
> 98 is greater than 97.
>
> There are 50 stars on the U.S. flag.
>
> Kansas is known as "The Sunflower State."
>
> The Pony Express began on April 3, 1860.
>
> John broke his arm when he fell from the tree.

Write two facts about yourself.

1. _____

2. _____

We listen for the *feelings* in a message because it's important to know how someone feels about what he's saying.

> **Feelings**
>
> happy   lonesome
>
> angry   frustrated

Write two feelings you sometimes have.

1. _____

2. _____

When you pay attention to both facts and feelings, you become a better listener. When you become a better listener, it's easier to understand other people. And we all know that understanding is the "name of the game!"

Fact or Feeling?

Read each statement below.   Then, identify the facts in each statement.   Identify possible feelings of the speaker, too.   The first one is done for you.

1.   Statement: "My motorcycle broke down yesterday and I had to take it to Motor Shack to be fixed."

Facts: *motorcycle broke down, yesterday, took it to Motor Shack*

Feelings: *unhappy, angry*

2.   Statement: "The Electric Earthworms are giving a concert at the City Arena next Saturday. I get to go because I won a free ticket from the radio station."

Facts: _____

_____

Feelings: _____

_____

3.   Statement: "I worked for three hours on my American History report last night.   It really looked great!   But guess what?   I left it on the school bus this morning."

Facts: _____

_____

Feelings: _____

_____

4.   Statement: "My boss gave me ten extra hours of work this week.   Now I'll have enough money to buy the stereo speakers I wanted.   The only problem is I have to work Saturday and Sunday, so I can't go to the movies with you."

Facts: _____

_____

Feelings: _____

_____

Listening Practice

Practice listening for facts and feelings in a REAL situation.   First, list two topics you could discuss with someone else.   Here are some ideas.

how old you should be to date	cafeteria food
getting a driver's permit	the kind of clothes you like
good movies or TV shows	your best vacation

Topic 1: _____

Topic 2: _____

Next, choose a partner.   Talk for two minutes about one of your topics.   Have your partner identify the facts and the feelings he hears on his worksheet.   Then, listen to your partner discuss a topic and do the same thing.

Topic: _____

Facts: _____

_____

_____

_____

_____

Feelings: _____

_____

_____

Paraphrasing

Another way to show someone that you are listening is to *paraphrase*, or restate, what the person said in your own words.   You have to listen closely to what someone is saying to be able to paraphrase his message.

A key point should be made here.   The paraphrase must be more *concise*, or shorter, than the original statement.

Here are some examples of paraphrases.   In each example, the second person is paraphrasing what the first person said.

Tim: "Boy, has this been a crazy week!   I had three tests at school and I worked 20 hours at the restaurant."

Luke: "You've really been busy."

Teacher: "Your class schedule will be different today because of our speaker.   You will have math class fourth period instead of fifth period.   You will have science class fifth period instead of fourth period."

Student: "Today, we have math class before we have science class."

Cindy: "We had a great time at the amusement park today. We rode all the rides and played a lot of games. Then, we ate dinner at Pizza King.   I'm exhausted!"

Hank: "Wow, no wonder you're so tired.   You did a lot of things!"

Did you notice that the paraphrases were short restatements of the facts?   It's not important to restate ALL of the facts.   But you do need to include enough information so the other person knows that you were listening.

Write a paraphrase for this statement.

Statement: "I spent most of yesterday working at my computer.   I'm trying to figure out a way to pay my bills and balance my checkbook."

Paraphrase: _____

_____

Paraphrasing Practice

Let's review.   A *paraphrase* is:

✔ used to show that you're listening

✔ a restatement of the facts

✔ more concise (shorter!)

> Last night my family and I ate at Jumbo Gumbo.   The food was very good.   We had fun watching Giggles the Clown make balloon animals for the little kids.

Choose the best paraphrase for the above statements.

_____ a.   Your family went somewhere and did something.

_____ b.   You and your family had fun when you ate at Jumbo Gumbo.

_____ c.   Giggles the Clown turned your family into balloon animals last night while you ate at the Jumbo Gumbo.

Now, write a paraphrase for each of these statements.

Statement: "Last summer my famiiy and I drove to the West Coast.   We visited my cousins who live near Los Angeles.   We stayed two weeks with them before we drove back home."

Paraphrase: _____

_____

Statement: "You will have a test this Friday.   I suggest that you review Chapters 5 through 7 and know the information on the three handouts.   It will be a 40-point test, but there won't be any essay questions."

Paraphrase: _____

_____

Statement: "Since 1953, United States' government agencies responsible for weather information have used girls' names to identify major tropical storms.   However, since 1979, boys' names have also been used to identify powerful storms."

Paraphrase: _____

_____

Say It Again

Practice paraphrasing in a REAL situation.   First, choose a partner.   Next, talk about a topic for 30 seconds.

Then, have your partner paraphrase what you said.   Take turns speaking and paraphrasing several times.   Here are some topics you might talk about.

making your favorite sandwich	sports
shopping	exercising
your classes	computers
getting along with parents	driving a car
smoking	weekend activities

After you practice paraphrasing several times, answer the questions below.

1. What topics did you talk about?

   _____

2. Was it easy or difficult to paraphrase what your partner said?   Why?

   _____

3. Did you feel your partner was listening to you?   How could you tell?

   _____

   _____

4. How does paraphrasing help you become a good listener?

   _____

   _____

Listening Quiz

Check what you've learned about listening by taking my *Listening Quiz*. Use the words in the box to complete the sentences. Good luck!

> show   question
> concentrate   ready
> signals   directions
> verbal   feelings
> paraphrase   argue

1. _____ on listening.

2. Verbal communication contains both facts and _____.

3. Asking a _____ lets the other person know that you're listening.

4. Get _____ to listen.

5. A _____ is a verbal restatement of a message.

6. _____ are clues from the teacher that tell you something is important.

7. Most directions are written or _____.

8. _____ that you are listening.

9. Try not to mentally _____ with the speaker.

10. A good student can follow _____.

Listening Practice

It's time to practice what you've learned!   Choose some activities you could do to practice your listening skills.   Use the list below to help you.

☐ Keep your desk and mind clear.   Be ready to listen.

☐ Sit upright at your desk.   Lean forward just a little.

☐ Make eye contact with your teachers and other speakers.

☐ Practice asking questions in two of your classes.

☐ Practice paraphrasing what your friends or teachers say.

☐ Look for important signals from your teachers.

☐ Whisper verbal directions to yourself.

☐ Make a mental picture when someone gives you verbal directions.

Now, write down the activities you try in the chart below.   Fill in the following information for each activity:

✔ Tell when you did the activity.

✔ Describe the activity.

✔ Explain how well you think the activity worked.

Date	Activity	How Well It Worked
February 14	Asked question in English class.	Helped me understand verbs better.

Clinton D. Fentonbenton's Amazing Facts

Amazing Fact #1:   On the average, most junior high students listen better than a ripe cabbage.

Amazing Fact #2:   The best listener of all time was Kevin "Ears" Washington.   Legend has it that from June 1, 1978 to September 10, 1988, he never once removed the headphones of his tape player from his ears.   When Kevin was 17, his parents were forced to have his headphones surgically removed.

Amazing Fact #3:   According to an old Bavarian superstition, it is considered bad luck to listen for a loud boom by placing your ear next to a lighted stick of dynamite.

Amazing Fact #4:   You can significantly decrease your listening skills by growing broccoli in your ears.

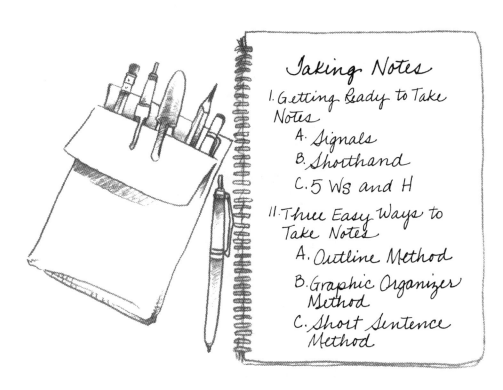

In this unit, you'll learn two important things — how to get ready to take notes and how to actually take them.   As you get ready to take notes, you'll learn:

✔ words that signal important information

✔ how to write down the important information by answering the 5W & H questions

✔ some "crash course" shorthand for writing your notes or other information

Then, you'll learn three ways to actually take notes as you listen or read:

✔ the outline method

✔ the graphic organizer method

✔ the short sentence method

I'll give you some handy dandy tips, too, on how to make your notes really help you "make the grade" in your classes.

That reminds me of my cousin Farkel.   Farkel Fentonbenton is an author.   He's writing a very down-to-earth book.   It's about a sky diver.

Signal Watch

Every teacher is different. (You know that.) Every teacher teaches differently. (You know that, too.) The trick is to find out as soon as possible how your teacher teaches and what your teacher thinks is important. If you know what the teacher expects from you, then getting a good grade should be easy.

In the unit on listening (Unit 3: Listening), I, Clinton D. Fentonbenton, gave you some really good information about signals. Remember, *signals* are signs that tell you the teacher is saying something important and you need to write it in your notes.

Here are some signals to help you take good notes:

✔ If the teacher writes information on the chalkboard, then you should write it in your notes.

✔ If the teacher says the information will be on the test, then it most likely will be, so write it in your notes.

✔ If the teacher says, "Now this is important . . ." or "Remember . . . ," then write the information in your notes.

✔ If the teacher talks a lot about certain information, then write it in your notes.

Here are more signal words and phrases your teacher might say or you might read in your textbooks.

Main Ideas	**Lists of Important Information**
Basically . . .	There are two parts to . . .
This is important because . . .	Follow these steps to . . .
In summary, . . .	Two groups of . . . are important to know.
The most important . . .	First, second, third . . .
In conclusion, . . .	Three characteristics or features are most common.
A key point is . . .	Two easy ways to . . .
The significance of this is . . .	There are several categories of . . .

With your class, list other signal words or phrases your teachers say or you read in your textbooks.

_____   _____

_____   _____

The Short Way

Do you find it hard to write down everything important your teacher says or that you read?   Well, I did until I learned to use shorthand.   *Shorthand* is a kind of writing that uses symbols and abbreviations instead of whole words.

Some schools offer classes in a specific style or method of shorthand.   If you are taking a shorthand class right now, you should probably use the style you are learning there.

If you're not using a specific style of shorthand, then you can use the ideas here.

Actually you can make up your own style of shorthand.   Any way you can shorten your writing time and still understand what you write is A-OK!

Here are some common words written in shorthand.

at	@
you	*u*
and	&
plus	+
can	*cn*
with	*w/ or w.*
without	*w/o*
equals	=
because	*b/c*
and so forth	*etc.*
for example	*e.g.*
about or regarding	*re:*

With your class, list other words you know how to write in shorthand or make up some new ones.

_____   _____

_____   _____

_____   _____

More Shorthand

You can shorten your writing by using initials, parts of words, numbers, or symbols. Here are more examples of shorthand.

United States	US	second	2nd
Canada	CAN	around	arnd
Middle East	ME	shorthand	shrthnd
street	st	words	wds
room	rm	John F. Kennedy	JFK
money	$	water	H_2O
more than	>	less than	<

Here's an example of a history student's notes:

The Amer Rev ws fought bet Amer & Engl. Amer won indep in 1776. We celebrt our indep frm Engl every Jul 4.

Write what you think the history student's notes say.

_____

_____

How would you write these words in shorthand? Remember, there's no correct answer here.

school	_____	history	_____	class	_____
science	_____	government	_____	book	_____
telephone	_____	work	_____	before	_____
chemistry	_____	information	_____	number	_____

Write these sentences in shorthand.

1. To take good notes in class, you must first be a good listener.

   _____

2. The number of representatives each state has in the House of Representatives is based on the state's population.

   _____

The 5 Ws & H

Suppose you just saw a great movie and wanted to tell your friends about it? What things would you remember? Most likely you would remember the main points of the movie.

The main points you remember about a movie are the same kinds of information you want to remember from a teacher's lecture or from your reading. These main points are called *The 5Ws & H.*

The 5Ws & H stand for *who, what, where, when, why,* and *how.* These words help you know the kind of information to listen for or to look for when you take notes.

Here's how The 5Ws & H work:

✔ First, write the words *who, what, where, when, why,* and *how* on your paper before you start listening or reading.

✔ Then, fill in the important information to answer a question when you hear it or read it.

✔ Remember, not everything you read or hear will have the information you need to answer all six questions.

Try The 5Ws & H on this paragraph.

Eagles are one of the largest and most powerful birds in the world. In North America, eagles are the second largest bird next to the California condor. Up close, eagles look fierce and proud, and thus, have become symbols of freedom and power. However, eagles aren't as fierce as they look. For example, eagles are timid hunters, and feed mainly on fish and dead animals. Eagles are careful to avoid danger. They are even afraid of human beings. In 1782, the United States chose the bald eagle as its national bird.

Who or what is the paragraph about? _____

What are eagles like? _____

Where are eagles found? _____

When did eagles become the United States' national bird? _____

Why was the eagle chosen as the national bird? _____

How do eagles symbolize freedom and power? _____

Three Easy Ways

Good morning, class. I will be your teacher today. My name is Mr. Clinton D. Fentonbenton.

You are now ready to learn how to take notes so you can study from them. First, I would like you to read the next five paragraphs very carefully.

Taking Notes

To be a successful student, it's important to take good, meaningful notes in class. No student can remember every word the teacher says about a topic or everything he reads. Note taking can help you remember things that are important.

Learning to take notes is not difficult once you learn how. There are three ways you can take notes.

The first way to take notes is to use the *outline method*. With the outline method, you organize important information into several *main topics*, or main subject areas. Each main topic contains *subtopics*, or groups of information about the main topic. Each subtopic then contains *details*, or extra information, that explain the subtopic.

The second way to take notes is called the *graphic organizer method*. A graphic organizer is a *visual map*, or a map you draw, that shows how important information goes together.

The third way to take notes is to simply write several short sentences that contain the important information. This is called the *short sentence method*.

How do you take notes?

_____

How do your classmates take notes?

_____

Three Kinds of Information

No matter what note-taking method you use, you need to listen or look for the most important information.   This important information includes:

✔ *Main topics*   the most important ideas or main subjects of what you hear or read

✔ *Subtopics*   additional information that explains the main topics

✔ *Details*   extra pieces of information that explain the subtopics

Here's the important information from the *Taking Notes* paragraphs on page 81.

Taking Notes

Main topic: Note taking is important.

    Subtopics: to be a successful student
                   to help remember important things

Main topic: Three ways to take notes

    Subtopic: outline method

        Details: main topics
                subtopics
                details

    Subtopic: graphic organizer method

        Details: draw a map of important information
                shows how information goes together

    Subtopic: short sentence method

        Details: write important information only
                write several short sentences

Outline Method

When you read or hear important information, you need to write it down in your notes so you can remember it. You can take notes in three easy ways — the outline method, the short sentence method, or the graphic organizer method.

Patti Pocketlint likes to use the outline method to take notes. First, she looks for the *main topics*, or major points of information. In the outline below, Patti has listed the main topics by the Roman numerals *I* and *II*.

Next, Patti looks for *subtopics*, or groups of information, that help explain the main topics. She has listed the subtopics as *A, B,* and *C* under the main topic they help explain.

Then, Patti looks for *details*, or extra pieces of information, that help explain the subtopics. Patti has listed the details by the numbers *1, 2,* and *3* under the subtopic they help explain.

Here are Patti's notes on the *Taking Notes* paragraphs on page 81.

Taking Notes
  I. Note taking is important
     A. to be a successful student
     B. to help remember important things

  II. Three ways to take notes
     A. outline method
        1. main topics
        2. subtopics
        3. details
     B. graphic organizer method
        1. draw a map of important information
        2. shows how information goes together
     C. short sentence method
        1. write important information only
        2. write several short sentences

Graphic Organizer

Donald Dripdrop likes to use a graphic organizer to take his notes. A *graphic organizer* is a drawing, or a visual map, that shows how important information goes together.

When you use a graphic organizer, you look for the main topics, the subtopics, and the details. A graphic organizer is like an outline, only the information is organized in a drawing. The ovals and lines you draw in a graphic organizer show how the main topics, subtopics, and details go together.

The kind of graphic organizer Donald used is called a *word web*. Here's Donald's word web.

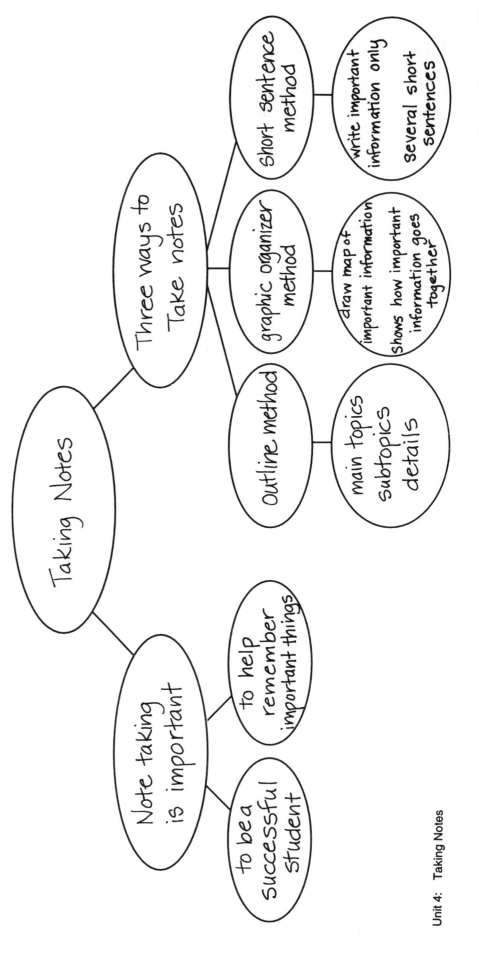

Short Sentence Method

Trixie Gumball likes to use the short sentence method to take notes.   She writes short sentences that include only the most important information.

Here are Trixie's notes on the information printed on page 81.   (Oh, you know, the stuff about the three methods of note taking!)

1. Note taking is important.

2. It helps you become a successful student.

3. There are three ways to take notes.

4. One way is the outline method.

5. Outline method is divided into main topics, subtopics, and details.

6. Another way is called the graphic organizer method.

7. Draw a map to show the important information.

8. The third way is called the short sentence method.

9. Sentences contain only important information.

Trixie's short sentences use just enough words to help her remember the important information.

Prepare to Paint

It's your turn to practice note taking.   First, read these paragraphs.

How to Paint a House

Have you ever helped someone paint a house?   House painting takes place in two main steps.

The first step in house painting is called preparation.   The painter makes sure that all of the supplies and equipment are at the house to be painted.   The painter must scrape off all the loose and peeling paint from the house.   After the scraping is done, the painter must wash the house to remove as much of the dirt as possible.

The second step is the actual painting.   Sometimes a *primer*, or first coat, of paint is applied before the finishing coat.   The painter usually paints from the top of the house down to the bottom.   Big areas are painted first.   The trim is usually painted last.   Neatness counts on this job.

Now, find the important information to include in notes on these paragraphs.

✔ Draw <u>one line</u> under the main topic.

✔ Draw <u>two lines</u> under each subtopic.

✔ Draw a ⬭circle⬭ around each detail.

Then, fill in the missing information in these notes using the outline method.

  I. House painting takes place in two steps

      A. _____

          1.   have all equipment at house

          2.   scrape loose and peeling paint

          3.   _____

      B. Second step is painting

          1.   apply primer coat first

          2.   paint from top to bottom

          3.   paint big areas first

          4.   _____

          5.   be neat

Painting Notes

Read the paragraphs about painting again on page 86. Then, take notes about the paragraphs using a graphic organizer method like a word web.

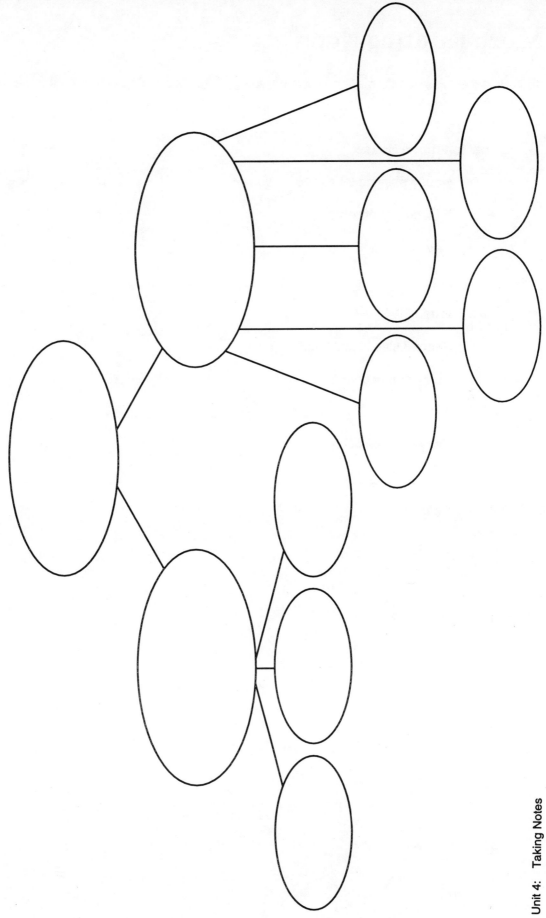

More Painting Notes

Now, fill in the missing information on the paragraphs about painting using the short sentence method.

How to Paint a House

1. House painting takes two steps.

2. First step is preparation.

3. Have all equipment.

4. _____

5. Wash the house.

6. Second step is painting.

7. Apply primer coat first.

8. _____

9. Paint big areas first.

10. _____

11. Be neat.

Note-taking Practice

Here are paragraphs you can use to practice note taking. Have someone else read the paragraphs to you or read them to yourself.

Remember to listen for or look for signal words and the answers to The 5Ws & H.

Then, take notes using the outline method, the graphic organizer method, or the short sentence method.

1. Ecology is a branch of biology that studies the relationship of living things to their environment. The study of ecology helps us understand the world and all its creatures. This is important because human survival depends on world-wide relationships. Changes all over the world affect everyone and everything in one way or another. Studying ecology helps us predict possible environmental problems, such as crop loss and animal overpopulation.

2. A cell is the basic unit of all life. All living things are made up of cells. The human body is made up of more than one trillion cells. Most cells are so small that they can only be seen under a microscope. Cells are alive — they "breathe," take in food, and get rid of wastes. Cells even *reproduce*, or create, other cells of their own kind.

3. Georgia is the largest state east of the Mississippi River. It is one of the leading manufacturing states in the southern United States. Georgia's size and its many industries have given Georgia the nickname "The Empire of the South." For many years, most of Georgia's citizens grew cotton for a living. When manufacturing expanded, cotton weaving became as important as growing the cotton itself. Today, *textile mills*, or mills that specialize in weaving, are Georgia's largest source of income.

4. In many ways, the human eye is similar to a camera. Both the eye and the camera need light to work properly. Neither the eye nor the camera can function well without light.

   The camera has a series of lenses to focus the *image,* or picture, properly. The human eye also has a lens for focusing images.

   Both the eye and the camera have parts that are photosensitive. *Photosensitive* means these parts react to light. In the camera, the photosensitive material is called the *film*. In the human eye, the photosensitive part is called the *retina*.

Note-taking Tips

Here are some tips for getting the most from your notes.

Tip 1: *Have your materials ready.* If you have your paper and pencil ready, you won't miss any important information your teacher gives you.

Tip 2: *Be ready to listen and ready to write.* Once you have your materials ready, make sure you're ready to listen and to write. Then, you'll pay attention better so you'll hear the important information you need to know.

Tip 3: *Write down the main topic as soon as you can.* By writing down the main topic, you'll know what other kinds of information to expect.

Tip 4: *Take notes using your own words.* If you write notes in your own words, you'll be more likely to understand and remember them.

Tip 5: *Be alert to important signals.* Get to know the signals your teachers give. If you know your teacher's signals, you'll know what information that teacher thinks is important to remember.

Tip 6: *Use shorthand.* You'll hear a lot of important information in class that you'll need to know. It's easier to write down all the important information if you have a shorthand system.

Tip 7: *Review your notes the same day.* If you review your notes the same day that you take them, you can keep the information fresh in your mind. You're also more likely to remember any other information you need to add to your notes.

Add your own tip for taking notes and explain how it helps.

Tip 8: _____

_____

_____

Quiz Time!

What do you remember about taking notes?   Answer the questions below to find out.

1. Why is note taking important for classroom success?

    _____

    _____

2. Match the shorthand with the word or phrase it represents.

e.g.	etc.	w/o	+	re:	w/

    _____ without   _____ plus

    _____ and so forth   _____ for example

    _____ with   _____ regarding or about

3. Put an X by the correct answer.   If you take notes by drawing a visual map of the information, you are using the:

    _____ a. outline method

    _____ b. short sentence method

    _____ c. graphic organizer method

4. Put an X by the correct answer.   If you take notes by organizing the information in several short sentences, you are using the:

    _____ a. outline method

    _____ b. short sentence method

    _____ c. graphic organizer method

5. List three signal words or phrases you might hear or read that tell you the information is important for you to write in your notes.

    _____

    _____

    _____

6. What are *The 5Ws & H*?   When should you use them?

    _____

    _____

Practice, Practice

It's time to practice what you've learned! Choose some activities you could do to practice taking notes. Use the list below to help you.

☐ Choose one note-taking method and use it in your classes for one week.

☐ Teach a note-taking method to a friend or classmate.

☐ With a friend or classmate, practice giving each other information for notes. Check to see if you're writing down the most important information.

☐ Choose a class and list all the signals your teacher uses to tell you which information is important. Share your list with someone else in the class and compare your ideas.

☐ Develop your own shorthand system. Use it to take notes in your classes. Make sure you can read it when you're done.

Now, write down the activities you try in the chart below. Fill in the following information for each activity:

✔ Tell when you did the activity.

✔ Describe the activity.

✔ Explain how well you think the activity worked.

Date	Activity	How Well It Worked
March 12	Used shorthand for history notes.	Great! Got all the information in my notes.

Clinton D. Fentonbenton's
Amazing Facts

Amazing Fact #1:   You can take notes in a music class, even if you can't read music notes.

Amazing Fact #2:   In 1948, the fastest note taker at Crocklock High School was Ima Leadwriter. She took notes so quickly, she had to use asbestos paper to keep from starting fires.

Amazing Fact #3:   In most schools, teachers like students to *take* notes, but they don't like students to *pass* notes!

Here's an old photograph of my room before I learned how to get organized.   Pretty scary, huh?   Soon after this picture was taken, I cleaned my room.   This is what I found:

> last week's pizza
> my long lost cousin
> a family of elves
> something that resembled my fourth-grade science project on mammals

In this unit, you'll learn that being organized will make studying easier for you.   You'll learn studying tips like:

✔ setting study goals

✔ planning your study breaks

✔ having your study materials and a quiet place to study

✔ avoiding interruptions

You'll learn how an assignment book can help you get your homework done right and on time.   You'll also learn the SMART method for reading your assignments.   And you'll learn some memory tricks to help you memorize everything you need to know.

Study-Skills Rating Scale

Howdy partner! Have you been hankerin' to know how good your study skills are? Well, shoot! Here's your chance to find out, buckaroo.

Complete *Clinton D. Fentonbenton's Cowpoke Study-Skills Rating Scale.* Now don't be a low-down polecat. Be sure to answer truthfully.

After each statement below, circle A, B, C, or D.

Clinton D. Fentonbenton's Cowpoke Study-Skills Rating Scale

almost always A	most of the time B	sometimes C	almost never D			
1. I keep my schoolbooks and papers in a certain place at home.			A	B	C	D
2. I keep my locker, my desk, and my room neat and organized.			A	B	C	D
3. Before I start my homework, I make a study plan.			A	B	C	D
4. I take breaks when I study.			A	B	C	D
5. I have a quiet place to study at home.			A	B	C	D
6. When I study at home, I try to avoid interruptions.			A	B	C	D
7. At home, I have the school supplies and reference materials I need.			A	B	C	D
8. I ask for help from my friends, family, or teachers if I get stuck on an assignment.			A	B	C	D
9. I end my study time with a brief review of what I've read or studied.			A	B	C	D
10. I study when I'm most wide awake.			A	B	C	D

Now, turn the page and see how you rate!

Study-Skills Rating Scale, *continued*

Find your total points by using the guidelines below.

Give yourself 4 points for each A you circled.   _____   X 4 = _____

Give yourself 3 points for each B you circled.   _____   X 3 = _____

Give yourself 2 points for each C you circled.   _____   X 2 = _____

Give yourself 1 point for each D you circled.   _____   X 1 = _____

Total Points = _____

Check the rating that matches your total points.

☐ 10 – 15 points   **Tenderfoot!**   I need to improve my study skills.

☐ 16 – 23 points   **Greenhorn!**   I'm getting better, but I still need to improve my study skills.

☐ 24 – 31 points   **Wrangler!**   I have good study skills.

☐ 32 – 40 points   **Trail Boss!**   I have excellent study skills.

Study Habits

Now that you know what kind of studier you are, you can think of ways to improve your study habits.   If you use the tips in this unit, you'll get more "study" out of your study time.

That means you can spend less time studying and more time "buddying"!

To get you thinking about how you study, answer these questions.   Be as honest as you can.

1. How much time do you usually study outside of class Monday through Friday?

    _____   minutes each day

2. How much time do you usually study on the weekend?

    _____   minutes on Saturday

    _____   minutes on Sunday

3. Where do you study?

    _____

4. Describe the place where you study.

    _____

    _____

5. Do you usually study alone or with a friend?   Why?

    _____

    _____

6. When do you usually study?   Why?

    _____

    _____

Discuss your answers with your classmates.   How do your study habits compare with theirs?

Study Tips

Here are five study tips you'll learn more about in this unit.   But first, let's find out what these study tips mean to you.   After each study tip, explain what it means to you.

Tip 1: *Plan your study time.*

_____

_____

Tip 2: *Take breaks.*

_____

_____

Tip 3: *Have the materials you'll need.*

_____

_____

Tip 4: *Have a place to work.*

_____

_____

Tip 5: *Avoid interruptions.*

_____

_____

Planning Time

It's a good idea to plan your study time by setting study goals. You can plan your study goals by following these tips:

✔ Decide what subject you will study first, second, third, and so on.

✔ Decide how long you will study before you take a break.

✔ Decide how long your breaks will be.

Here are Dagwood Dogwhistle's homework assignments.

○	Math – page 52 do problems 1–15.
○	Biology – Review Chapter 5 for quiz.
○	English – Read pages 88–90. Do questions 1–5 on pg. 91.

What do you think Dagwood's study goals should be? Why?

_____

_____

Now, fill in the chart below with your study goals. Use your real assignments.

Order	Subject	Length of Study Period	Length of Break
1			
2			
3			
4			

Taking Breaks

For me, Clinton D. Fentonbenton, taking breaks is the best part of studying.   After reading textbooks, I need a break.   After doing algebra problems, I need a break.   After writing essays, I need a break. Let's face it, sometimes I study just so I can take a break!

I bet you think that taking a break from studying is easy.   I bet you think taking a break means you just stop studying for a while.   Well . . . you're right.

But, there is a right way and a wrong way to take study breaks.   For example, going to the refrigerator for some ice cream is okay.   Going to the movies for some popcorn is NOT okay.

When you study at home, you should take two kinds of study breaks.

In-Chair Brain Break	Out-of-Chair Body Break
✔ take every 15 minutes	✔ take every 30 minutes
✔ remain seated	✔ stand up, walk around
✔ 30 seconds in length	✔ 5 minutes in length
✔ stretch and yawn	✔ get food, use the bathroom
✔ daydream about something fun (but only for 30 seconds)	✔ do something away from the study area
✔ go right back to your work	✔ go right back to your work

You have been studying hard.   Your brain is about to melt down.   Describe what you would do during a five-minute, out-of-chair body break.

_____

_____

_____

School Supplies

When you study, it's important to have the school supplies you need with you.   Read the list of school supplies below.

Think about the supplies you use when you study and how often you use them.   Then, write each item in the correct column.

pencil sharpener	paste	workbooks
index cards	paper clips	encyclopedias
pen	yo-yo	notebooks
eraser	stapler	clock
pencil	glue	ruler
assignment book	scissors	staples
felt-tip markers	spare tire	paper
tape	bookmark	globe
monkey wrench	textbooks	folders
highlighter	crayons	dictionary
maps	lamp	wastebasket

I use often when I study	I sometimes use when I study	I never use when I study

Check your school supplies at home.   What supplies do you need?

_____

Where do you keep your school supplies? _____

A Place to Study

Where you study is very important.   Your place of study should be:

  ✔ comfortable, but also business-like

  ✔ well lit so you can see your work

  ✔ free from clutter and things that can distract you

  ✔ quiet enough for you to concentrate on your work

If you need to write when you study, work at a table or a desk so you can write more easily.

If you need to read something, pick a place where you're most comfortable and can pay attention. Some students like to read at a desk or a table.   Other students like to read while lying on the floor or sitting in a rocker or a recliner.   Pick a place that's right for you.

Describe or draw a picture of your ideal study area below.   Describe or draw the furniture, the school supplies, the place where you read, the noise level, the lighting, and so on.   Then, explain why this is a good place for you to study.

_____

_____

_____

_____

_____

Do Not Disturb

When you study at home, it's important to avoid *interruptions*, or things that keep you from paying attention to your studying.   If you can avoid interruptions, you can concentrate better.

If you are not interrupted while you study, you will also be more *productive*.   Being productive means you will get more schoolwork done in less time. The quality of your work will also be better.

To avoid interruptions, you may need help from your family.   Here are some ideas:

- ✔ Ask your family for privacy while you're studying.   In other words, ask them to leave you alone until you're done studying.

- ✔ Ask your family to answer the phone and take messages when you're studying.   You can return your calls later.

- ✔ Ask your family to keep the noise level down so you can concentrate only on studying.

Have I told you how noisy it can be at my house?   The other day the airport called to ask us to be quiet.   They said they were having trouble hearing the jets land!

Fill in the chart below.   First, list the kinds of interruptions you sometimes have when studying.   Then, tell what you could do to avoid each interruption.

Interruption	How to Avoid

Assignment Notebook

Hello there!   This is a commercial for assignment notebooks.

If you use an assignment notebook, you will probably remember to do your assignments.

If you don't use an assignment notebook, you will probably forget to do your assignments.

If you forget to do your assignments, you will get poor grades and your mother will make you eat beets every night of the week.   Thank you for listening!

Here is Gary Greatgrade's assignment notebook.   Gary always remembers his assignments because he's organized.   Way to go Gary!

O	Class: *Science*		Today's Date: *October 16*
	Assignment: *Read pgs. 106-111. Finish light experiment.*		Due Date: *October 18*
O	Class: *Math*		Today's Date: *October 17*
	Assignment: *Pg. 88, do odd # problems.*		Due Date: *October 18*
O	Class: *English*		Today's Date: *October 17*
	Assignment: *Test - study with Mark and Jacquile.*		Due Date: *October 20*
Notes:	*Monday, October 20 - Play practice starts. Class photos.*		

Notice that Gary has written all of the subjects he has assignments in.   Gary has also written very specific instructions about each assignment, like the pages, the problem or question numbers, and the date each assignment is due.   Gary even has room to write other important notes to himself.

Using the page from Gary's assignment notebook, follow these directions:

   ✔ Draw a rectangle around the date.

   ✔ Put a star beside each subject.   Draw a line under each assignment.

   ✔ Then, circle the notes Gary has written to himself.

Homework Time

Here are tips for using your assignment notebook:

✔ Take your assignment notebook to every class.

✔ Write down each assignment as soon as you hear it.

✔ Read your assignment notebook at the end of the school day so you know which books and materials you need to take home.

✔ Read your assignment notebook when you get ready to do your homework so you understand the assignment.

✔ Check off or draw a line through each assignment as you complete it.

Practice writing specific assignments on the page below.   Use your own real assignments for the day or make up some examples.   Write any other activities or reminders in the *Notes* section.

○	Class:	Today's Date:
	Assignment:	Due Date:
	Class:	Today's Date:
	Assignment:	Due Date:
○	Class:	Today's Date:
	Assignment:	Due Date:
	Class:	Today's Date:
	Assignment:	Due Date:
○	Class:	Today's Date:
	Assignment:	Due Date:
Notes:		

The SMART Way

Hey! Do you want to be a smart reader? I mean, do you want to be able to read any textbook and be smart about it? Well, I think I can help.

I'm here to tell you about a different way to read textbooks called the *SMART* way. Please pay attention while I explain.

There are five easy steps to reading and understanding any of your textbooks. Each of the five steps starts with a letter (S.M.A.R.T.). Pretty "smart," huh? Here's what each letter means.

S is for **Scope**   *Scope it out.* Browse through the reading material. Look at the pictures. Read the captions. Notice the charts and graphs. Read the titles. Notice the headings in bold print. Take time to read the questions at the end of the chapter, too.

M is for **Measure**   *Measure your reading.* Decide where you will start reading. Decide where you will stop reading. Decide on the amount of reading that's comfortable for you.

A is for **Ask**   *Ask questions.* Ask yourself questions about what you are going to read. What is it about? What are the main points? Are there lots of new vocabulary words? Is the reading full of dates or people's names?

R is for **Read**   *Read it.* Read at a nice, steady pace. If you don't understand something, keep going. Mark it and come back to that part later. When you are reading, either read aloud or try to make it sound in your head as if someone is reading the words to you. Take notes on your reading, too, if it will help you.

T is for **Test**   *Test your understanding.* Put into your own words what you know about what you just read. Whisper to yourself all the details you can remember or write the details down. When you think you understand what you read, move on to the next section of reading.

Reading SMART

Before you do this page, review the information on page 106. Make sure you understand what it means to be a SMART reader.

Now, put into your own words what these five steps mean to you. Think of what you do for each step as you read an assignment.

S

Scope it out.

_____

_____

M

Measure your reading.

_____

_____

A

Ask questions.

_____

_____

R

Read it.

_____

_____

T

Test your understanding.

_____

_____

With a classmate, practice the SMART way to read using one of your textbooks. Then, quiz each other over the same material to see what you've learned. Write a summary of what you learned.

Practice the SMART way to read every day.

Memory Tricks

Earlier in this chapter you learned how to be a SMART reader. The word *SMART* is a *mnemonic* (nĭ-mon-ick) *device*, or a memory trick. SMART represents the first letters of the first words of five sentences. These five sentences remind you how to read an assignment in a textbook.

Fill in the first words of these sentences describing the SMART way to read.

S _____ it out.

M _____ your reading.

A _____ questions.

R _____ it.

T _____ your understanding.

Now, let's suppose you're going on a camping trip with your friends. You have been put in charge of bringing these items:

onions	pots	tent	stove

Because you don't want to forget these camping items, you memorize them by using a mnemonic device called *Make A Word*. Here's how you do it:

✔ First, write down the items you want to remember.

✔ Second, underline the first letter of each item on the list.

✔ Third, try to make a word out of the underlined letters.
  If you can't make a real word, make a word that is almost a real word.

  T is for tent.
  O is for onions.
  P is for pots.
  S is for stove.

When you get ready for the camping trip, you just remember the word *TOPS*. Each letter in the word *TOPS* stands for one of the items on your camping list.

What other words can you make from the letters T, O, P, S?

Memory Tricks, *continued*

Since the order of the camping items is not important, you can scramble the letters any way you want.

But don't rearrange items if it's important to know them in a particular sequence, like the order of the nine planets.

Write your own Make A Word memory trick for the four basic math processes.

Addition	Subtraction	Multiplication	Division

_____

_____

_____

_____

Think of at least two more ways you can use the Make A Word mnemonic device for your schoolwork or for something you need to do at home.   Write your memory tricks below.

1. _____

_____

2. _____

_____

Silly Sentences

Another type of mnemonic device is called the *Silly Sentence* method. You can use this method if the Make A Word method doesn't work. Here's how you do it:

- ✔ First, underline the beginning letter of each item you want to memorize.

- ✔ Second, think of words that start with the letters you underlined.

- ✔ Third, use those words to make a sentence.

Your sentences may be a bit silly, but that's okay. If you can't make a complete sentence, try to make a phrase.

Here's an example of what I mean. When I worked at my Uncle Clark's garage, it was my job to check all of the fluid levels for every car to be serviced. I needed to check six fluid levels — battery, oil, antifreeze, brakes, transmission, and windshield washer.

If I forgot to check all six things, I didn't get paid. So I made up this silly sentence to help me remember:

This always brings wanted oily bucks.

The first letter of each word in my silly sentence stands for the first letter of the fluid levels I needed to check.

This stands for Transmission.

Always stands for Antifreeze.

Brings stands for Brakes.

Wanted stands for Windshield Washer.

Oily stands for Oil.

Bucks stands for Battery.

The Silly Sentence method really helped me. I always got paid, but not with oily bucks!

Make a silly sentence to remember the six parts to a computer system.

| monitor | printer | keyboard | computer | mouse | drive |

_____

_____

Grandma's Rule

Grandma Fentonbenton's Rule: First you work, then you play.

First, do this exercise.   Write the correct word in the blank.   The answer is jumbled below the blank.

1. The organized student keeps her work space _____ free.
    cutlert

2. All students should carry and use an _____ notebook.
    sgniastenm

3. I like to do my homework _____ so I can enjoy the rest of my day.
    yeral

4. When you study, you should avoid _____.
    ntierrtionups

5. Take an _____ after you study for thirty minutes.
    otu-fo-hciar doby kbera

Now, have fun solving the Word Find.   Circle the following study materials.

pencil	notebook	paper	markers
ruler	scissors	glue	dictionary
tape	eraser		

L	S	E	W	J	A	W	M	Q	E	N	U	Q	E	D
W	I	P	P	A	P	E	R	U	E	N	N	P	K	R
C	V	O	D	B	X	C	L	Z	O	Z	A	N	Y	V
C	I	S	P	P	Q	G	Y	E	N	T	C	H	Z	M
A	X	D	J	S	N	Z	Y	P	Y	R	S	P	Y	E
W	E	V	I	Y	C	T	I	K	S	R	O	E	M	I
H	B	B	A	C	G	I	O	T	E	A	A	N	Y	D
P	H	V	B	D	T	O	S	K	M	E	M	C	T	D
X	V	E	D	A	B	I	R	S	I	W	O	I	E	U
G	Q	H	K	E	O	A	O	N	O	R	C	L	R	W
R	J	A	T	K	M	V	Y	N	B	R	A	O	A	O
E	C	O	F	M	C	G	F	O	A	A	S	L	S	G
C	N	Y	A	F	A	A	P	C	I	R	D	H	E	A
P	E	V	Y	R	E	H	L	J	W	Q	Y	A	R	X
R	U	L	E	R	D	I	A	S	D	G	N	O	R	G

Studying Practice

Howdy-do, buckaroo!   I bet you enjoyed yourself immensely when you took *Clinton D. Fentonbenton's Cowpoke Study-Skills Rating Scale* at the beginning of this unit.   Now, it's time to practice what you've learned.   Choose some activities you could do to practice studying.   Use the list below to help you.

- [ ] Decide on a certain time you will study every day.   Then, stick to your schedule.

- [ ] Arrange a certain place in your home where you can concentrate on your studying.

- [ ] Talk to your family about helping you avoid interruptions.

- [ ] Think of three fun things you can do during a five-minute out-of-chair body break.

- [ ] Buy and use an assignment notebook.

- [ ] Try to reach your study goals every day for one week.

- [ ] Try using the *SMART* way to read one of your textbooks.

- [ ] Use the *Make A Word* or *Silly Sentence* method to memorize information for a test.

- [ ] Check your school supplies and buy what you need.

Now, write down the activities you try in the chart below.   Fill in the following information for each activity:

- ✔ Tell when you did the activity.

- ✔ Describe the activity.

- ✔ Explain how well you think the activity worked.

Date	Activity	How Well It Worked
March 26	Started using an assignment notebook.	I've done all of my homework this week.

Clinton D. Fentonbenton's Amazing Facts

Amazing Fact #1: Dennis Doolittle, of Columbus, Ohio, reports that it's not his fault he got an F in history.   He claims the teacher kept asking him about things that happened before he was born.

Amazing Fact #2: In 1903, Congress passed a law making it mandatory for all students to eat bananas while they study.   Students all over America liked this law.   They found it a-peel-ing.

Amazing Fact #3: Nora Nodder has this sign on her bedroom door: *If you come into my room and find me studying, please wake me up!*

Amazing Fact #4: Bobbie Bagfish likes to study while taking a bath.   But everytime she gets into the tub the phone rings.   On March 1, 1988, she officially complained to the telephone company.   The very next day, the phone company came out and took away Bobbie's bathtub.

In the future, students won't have to take tests. The teacher will teach all week. Then on Friday, each student will be hooked up to the Brain-O-Meter. The Brain-O-Meter will show how much the student learned that week.

Just think, no more tricky true/false questions. No more "all of the above" multiple-choice questions. No more difficult essay questions. No more tests!

Dream on! For now, you still have to take tests. The information in this unit will help you get better grades on those tests, though. In this unit, you will learn about test taking in two parts:

✔ how to get ready for tests   ✔ how to take tests

You'll learn why it's important to ask specific questions about the kind of test you'll be taking. You'll also learn how to study for a test.

Once you're ready for the test, you'll learn how to actually take it. You'll learn tips for answering many kinds of questions including:

✔ fill-in-the-blank questions   ✔ matching questions

✔ true/false questions   ✔ essay questions

✔ multiple-choice questions

You'll also learn tips to help you do well on any kind of test.

Speaking of tests, did you hear about Moose Bullhammer? He asked the school nurse if he could do extra credit work for her — to make up for the eye test he flunked!

Test-Taking Rating Scale

Space Station Alpha-One to Earth. Come in Earth. This is Space Cadet Clinton D. Fentonbenton calling. My computer log says it's time to check out your test-taking skills.

Prepare to take *Clinton D. Fentonbenton's Rocket-to-the-Top Test-Taking Rating Scale.* Red alert! Red alert! Only input answers that are true for you. End of message. Beep!

After each statement, circle A, B, C, or D.

Clinton D. Fentonbenton's Rocket-to-the-Top Test-Taking Rating Scale

almost always A	most of the time B	sometimes C	almost never D
1. I find out from my teacher what kind of test I'll be taking.			A B C D
2. I begin studying for a test several days ahead of time.			A B C D
3. I use my notes when I study for a test.			A B C D
4. When I study for a test, I review information from many sources, like my notes, handouts, and reading assignments.			A B C D
5. I try to guess what questions the teacher will ask on the test.			A B C D
6. I review study material with a friend or a parent.			A B C D
7. I write down important dates, names, or phrases to remember for my tests.			A B C D
8. I study in a quiet place.			A B C D
9. I read all test directions and test questions carefully.			A B C D
10. I check my answers before I hand in my test.			A B C D

Now, turn the page and see how you rate!

Test-Taking Rating Scale, *continued*

Now, find your total points by using the guidelines below.

Give yourself 4 points for each A you circled. _____ X 4 = _____

Give yourself 3 points for each B you circled. _____ X 3 = _____

Give yourself 2 points for each C you circled. _____ X 2 = _____

Give yourself 1 point for each D you circled. _____ X 1 = _____

Total Points = _____

Check the rating below that matches your total points.

☐ 10 – 15 points **In Outer Space!** I need to improve my test-taking skills.

☐ 16 – 23 points **Maintaining Orbit!** I'm getting better, but I still need to improve my test-taking skills.

☐ 24 – 31 points **Zoom to the Moon!** I have good test-taking skills.

☐ 32 – 40 points **Rocket to the Top!** I have excellent test-taking skills.

Getting Ready

One of the most important ways to get ready for a test is to ask your teacher questions about it. You will be better prepared if you know exactly what to expect. Ask your teacher questions like these.

1. *When is the test?* Write the date, time, and place for your test in your assignment book.

2. *What will the test cover?* Ask which pages or chapters in your textbook will be included on the test. Ask if information from any handouts, assignments, or other sources will be included on the test. Write this information in your assignment book.

3. *What kind of a test will it be?* Ask your teacher if the test questions will be fill-in-the-blank, multiple choice, true/false, matching, or essay. The test could have many types of questions.

4. *How many questions will be on the test?* You'll have a better idea how long the test will take and how much each question will be worth.

5. *Will there be a review day or a study sheet before the test date?* Ask your teacher if she'll provide study help before the test so you can plan how best to prepare.

If you know the answers to these questions, then there should be no major surprises on the day of the test — except maybe the surprise you'll have when you see how good your grade is!

With a classmate, think of other questions you could ask your teacher to help you get ready for a test.

1. _____

2. _____

3. _____

Studying for Tests

Your teacher announces there will be a test. This doesn't surprise you. Every teacher gives tests. In a polite manner, you ask your teacher a few important questions about the test. You now know:

✔ the date, time, and place of the test

✔ what material the test will cover

✔ the number and types of questions on the test

You're feeling good. But suddenly you realize that you have to do more. Please take this one-point quiz.

Quiz

1. What do you do next?

   a. You panic. (You run screaming from the classroom.)

   b. You become depressed. (You cry for the next four days.)

   c. You get angry. (You plan to get even with somebody for something.)

   d. You get organized. (You plan how you will study for the test.)

Studying for a test can be a bit nerve-racking. I mean, you wonder if you're studying the right stuff. You worry about remembering what you studied. And then, you have to wait to find out how you did on the test. Wow! Studying for a test can make a person goofy!

I, Clinton D. Fentonbenton, am here to tell you that studying for a test doesn't have to be so painful. Here are five ways you can do better on your tests.

Five Ways to Study for a Test

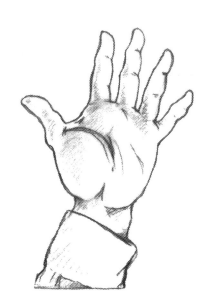

1. *Develop a study plan.* Decide when, where, and what you will study. Plan to study for the test every day. Make sure you have all the study materials you need.

2. *Review your notes.* Do you have new information to add to your notes? Do you need to rewrite your notes? Do you need to get any missing notes from a classmate or your teacher?

3. *Read the textbook.* When you read the textbook, be sure to use the SMART way. (Look back at Unit 5: Studying to review the SMART way.)

4. *Use other resources.* Get information from classroom bulletin boards, models, experiments, films, worksheets, class discussions, and your classmates. Write down the main ideas of the information you get from these resources.

Studying for Tests, *continued*

5. *Know what your teacher emphasized.* Identify lessons your teacher seemed to *emphasize*, or put a lot of importance on. Did your teacher spend more time on a particular lesson? Did your teacher seem more excited about a particular lesson?

With a group of three or four classmates, choose a class you have in common. Then, discuss how you could study for a big test in that class.

How do you study that's the same as your classmates?

_____

_____

How do you study that's different from your classmates?

_____

_____

Taking Tests

My biology teacher, Mrs. Greengrow, announced there would be a 20 question multiple-choice test on Friday.   I used the *Five Ways to Study for a Test* on pages 118-119 to get ready for it.   Guess what? I got my highest grade ever in biology!

Plan what you'll do for a test you have to take.   Answer the following questions to help you prepare. Look back at the *Five Ways to Study for a Test* for ideas.

1. What class is your test in?   _____

2. What do you know about the test, like when it will be, the kinds of questions, etc.?

   _____

   _____

3. What will your study plan be?

   _____

   _____

4. What notes will you review?

   _____

   _____

5. What parts of the textbook do you need to read?   How will you use the SMART method?

   _____

   _____

6. What other resources will you use?

   _____

   _____

7. What did your teacher emphasize in class lessons?

   _____

   _____

Test-Taking Tips

Here are four more tips for studying for a test.

1. *Pretend you are the teacher.* Make a list of the questions you would ask if you were the teacher. Know the answers to your questions.

2. *Use review sheets.* If your teacher gives you a practice sheet or a review sheet, be sure to study it. Know the information on all the review sheets or practice sheets your teacher hands out.

3. *Test yourself.* Ask a friend or family member to drill you on specific facts and vocabulary words.

4. *Form a study group.* Organize a study group with two or three other students. Be sure to include only those students who are serious about studying. Discuss the material from your class and ask each other questions.

Answer these essay questions. Be sure to explain your answers completely.

1. Why do you think it's important to have a study plan?

   _____

   _____

   _____

2. What would you do if you were the leader of a study group?

   _____

   _____

   _____

Fill in the Blank

The first part of this unit showed you several ways to get ready for a test. The second part of this unit will help you understand how to take a test.

To take a test, it's important to know how to answer the different kinds of questions that might be on it. You'll find tips on the next few pages to help you answer many kinds of questions.

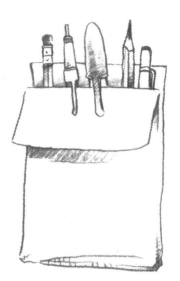

The first kind of questions you'll learn about are fill-in-the-blank questions. Some students call them "fill in the blankety-blank-blank" questions!

Fill-in-the _____ questions look for short, simple answers. The correct answer will usually be a single word. If more words are needed for an answer, the question will usually have more than one blank.

For fill-in-the-blank questions, you will sometimes have a list of words to choose from. Other times, you have to think of the word or words yourself.

Here are tips for answering fill-in-the-blank questions.

1. *Look over the test and begin with the easiest questions first.* Circle the number beside the questions you skip. Go back to the questions you skipped before you move on to the next section.

2. *Try to get clues from the other words in the sentence.* These clues may help you decide which word might fill in the blank.

3. *Look at the length of the blank or the number of blanks.* Sometimes the length of the blank or the number of blanks can help you figure out what word or words fill in the blank.

4. *If you have a list of words to choose from, cross off a word when you use it.* A word is usually used only once unless your teacher or the directions tell you it can be used again.

5. *Read the statement with your answer to see if it makes sense.*

Fill in the Blank, *continued*

Practice with these fill-in-the-blank questions.   One word is used twice.

ophthalmologist	iris	vision
sense	color	shape
color blindness	two	inherited

1. It is important for us to take care of our eyes so we have good _____.

2. The human eye is one of our most valuable _____ organs.

3. The _____ is the colored part of the eye.

4. Our eyes allow us to see the _____ and _____ of things.

5. If someone is not able to tell the difference between the colors he sees, he may have

   an _____ problem called _____ _____.

6. The doctor who examines your eyes is called an _____.

7. It is a good idea to have your eyes examined every _____ years to check

   your _____.

True or False?

Another kind of test question is a true/false question. Take this one-point true/false quiz.

Quiz

1. True   False   Many students like true/false tests.

The answer is *true*. Many students do like true/false questions on tests. Students think that if they don't know the answer, they at least have a chance at guessing the correct answer.

It is very easy to be tricked or confused by true/false questions, so be careful. Here are three tips to help you answer true/false questions.

1. *Read the entire statement before you decide if it is true or false.* Sometimes the first part of the statement will be true, but the second part will be false.

   If any part of the statement is false, then the entire statement is false. Read the statement very carefully.

2. *Statements that use the words* always *or* never *are usually false.* Because there are exceptions to most rules, *never* and *always* are rarely used in true statements.

3. *Decide if the statement is a fact or an opinion.* A *fact* can be proven. Facts are always true.

   An *opinion* is someone's feelings about something. If the statement is an opinion, then it is false.

Practice with these true/false statements. Write the word *True* or *False* in the blank.

1. _____ Birds always fly south for the winter.

2. _____ A popular event of the Olympic Games is swimming.

3. _____ The first recorded Olympic Games were held in Greece.

4. _____ Many birds fly south for the winter.

5. _____ True or false questions are sometimes tricky.

6. _____ The Olympic Games are held every four years in the United States.

7. _____ If you see the word *never* in a true or false statement, it will always be false.

8. _____ True/False questions are the easiest to answer.

9. _____ The *D* in Clinton D. Fentonbenton's name stands for *Derwood*.

Multiple Choice

Many teachers use multiple-choice questions on their tests. What's so tricky about multiple-choice questions is that you have so many answers to choose from!

Students who prepare for a test usually do well on multiple-choice tests. Here are some tips for answering multiple-choice questions.

1. *Be sure you understand the directions.* Do you circle the correct answer? Do you write the letter or number of the correct answer in a space?

2. *Read each question carefully so you know what you're being asked.*

3. *Read each possible answer before you start to think about the correct answer.*

4. *Eliminate the incorrect answers.* Put a line through them or check them off to help you leave only the answers that might be correct.

5. *Don't spend a lot of time on a question that has you stumped.* Circle that one and come back to it later.

6. *Be careful with* none of the above *and* all of the above *answers.* Choose *all of the above* when *all* of the answers are correct. Choose *none of the above* when *none* of the answers are correct.

Practice with these multiple-choice questions. Print the correct letter in the space provided.

_____ 1. The organ that pumps blood is called the:

    a. lung
    b. heart
    c. brain
    d. kidney

_____ 2. The system that turns food into fuel for the body to use is the:

    a. circulatory system
    b. skeletal system
    c. respiratory system
    d. digestive system

_____ 3. The nervous system is made up of the:

    a. heart and lungs
    b. brain and heart
    c. brain and spinal cord
    d. heart and spinal cord

_____ 4. The skeletal system is made up of:

    a. blood vessels
    b. bones
    c. arteries
    d. intestines

Multiple Choice, *continued*

_____ 5. Someday, Clinton D. Fentonbenton would like to be a:

      a. professional wrestler
      b. world class complainer
      c. jelly bean picker
      d. travel agent

_____ 6. Which of the following are *oceans*?

      a. Pacific
      b. Atlantic
      c. Arctic
      d. all of the above

_____ 7. Which *continent* is in the Northern Hemisphere?

      a. Germany
      b. Bolivia
      c. Greenland
      d. none of the above

_____ 8. Which is a part of the human ear?

      a. anvil
      b. stirrup
      c. hammer
      d. all of the above
      e. none of the above

Matching Questions

You might also see matching questions on a test. A matching question usually asks you to match a statement or a definition from one column with a word or phrase from another column. You then write your answer as a number or a letter.

Here are tips for answering matching questions.

1. *Check off or cross out each answer as you use it.* This will help you know which answers are left.

2. *Ask your teacher if any answers are used more than once.* Sometimes you can use the same answer again.

3. *Check how many answers you have to choose from.* Sometimes there are more answers than there are questions.

4. *Reread the statement with your answer to see if it makes sense.*

Practice with these matching questions.

Match the word to its definition.

_____ 1. democracy

_____ 2. dictatorship

_____ 3. monarchy

   a. government by an absolute ruler

   b. government by a king or queen

   c. government by the people

Match the city with the state. One answer is used twice.

_____ 4. Boston

_____ 5. Chicago

_____ 6. St. Louis

_____ 7. Orlando

_____ 8. Los Angeles

_____ 9. Denver

_____ 10. Des Moines

_____ 11. San Francisco

_____ 12. Tulsa

_____ 13. New York City

   a. California

   b. Colorado

   c. New York

   d. Oklahoma

   e. New Mexico

   f. Massachusetts

   g. Illinois

   h. Missouri

   i. Iowa

   j. Ohio

   k. Florida

   l. Kansas

Essay Questions

Students probably fear essay questions more than any other type of question. That's because you REALLY need to know the material from your class to be able to answer an essay question.

True/false, multiple-choice, matching, and fill-in-the-blank questions require you to know specific pieces of information.

Essay questions require you to understand *main ideas*, or important points, of what you've been learning. So, when you are studying for a test that will have essay questions, you need to keep asking yourself, "What is the main idea of this material?"

Even if you only know a little bit about the subject of the essay question, you have a chance to earn some points. Some points are better than no points. How well you answer essay questions depends on how well you prepare for the test.

Here are tips to help you answer essay questions.

1. *Read all the questions and directions carefully.* Do you have a choice of questions? Do you have a *word limit*, or certain number of words you must write? Do any questions have two parts to answer?

2. *Be aware of your time limits.* Notice how many questions you have to answer. Then, figure out how much time you have to answer each one.

3. *Before you begin your answer, write down or outline the main points you want to include in your answer.* Write your ideas on scrap paper, in the margins of the test, or on the back of the page.

4. *After you have written your answer, check it.* Does your answer make sense? Did it answer the question? Did you use correct punctuation, capitalization, and spelling?

Practice with this essay question.

Why are essay questions harder to answer than true/false, multiple-choice, matching, or fill-in-the-blank questions? Explain your answer in 50 words or more.

_____

_____

_____

_____

_____

_____

Real Test Questions

Practice writing test questions for a test you'll be taking.   First, choose a class where you'll be taking a test soon.

Next, write a fill-in-the-blank, true/false, matching, multiple-choice, and essay question for the material you'll be tested on.   Be able to answer your own questions.

Then, exchange your paper with someone else taking the same class and take each other's "test." Remember the tips for answering each type of question.   Writing possible test questions might just help you do well on the real test!

Which class do you have a test in?   _____

What information will be covered on the test?   _____

_____

Write a fill-in-the-blank question.

1. _____

_____

Write a true/false question.

2. _____

_____

Write a matching question.

3. _____

_____

Write a multiple-choice question.

4. _____

_____

Write an essay question.

5. _____

_____

More Test Tips

Here are some general tips for taking tests.

1. *Make sure your name is on the test.*

2. *Try to be calm.*   Take a couple of deep breaths before you begin and occasionally while you are taking the test.

3. *Before beginning, look at the test to see what kinds of questions there are.*   Look at how many questions there are, too.

4. *Read all the directions carefully.*

5. *If the answer sheet is separate from the rest of the test, check that you are putting your answers in the right places.*

6. *If you get stuck on one question, circle it and move on to the next question.*   Don't spend too much time on any one question.   Come back to the circled questions later.

7. *Be sure to write neatly.*   There is no point in putting down the correct answer if no one can read it.

8. *If you're not sure of the correct answer to a multiple-choice or matching question, decide which answers are incorrect.*   Then, make your best choice from the answers that are left.

9. *Review your answers on the test.*   Make sure you didn't skip any parts of the test and that you followed directions correctly.

Add a tip of your own and explain why it works.

10. _____

_____

_____

Testing Practice

Here is a practice test.   Read the directions carefully.   Have fun!

Fill-in-the-blank

Fill in each blank with the correct word.

1. A blacksmith might make _____ for a horse.

2. The planet Saturn has colorful _____ around it.

3. Animals that have disappeared from the earth are said to be _____.

4. A scientist uses a _____ to see a single-celled organism.

True or False

Circle *True* or *False.*

5.   True   False   All boys like to watch football games.

6.   True   False   March is the third month of the year.

7.   True   False   Learning can be fun.

8.   True   False   Astronomy is the study of planets and stars.

9.   True   False   There are thirty days in each month.

10.   True   False   Unorganized students are always poor spellers.

Matching

Write the correct letter in the blank next to the definition.

_____   11.   the part an actor plays   a.   clarify

_____   12.   orderly; in a systematic manner   b.   lesson

_____   13.   to make clear   c.   organized

_____   14.   to promise   d.   prefer

                                e.   role

                                f.   guarantee

Testing Practice, *continued*

Multiple Choice

Write the correct letter in the blank.

_____ 15. Small lumps of ice that fall from the sky are called:

        a. vapor
        b. hail
        c. snow
        d. rain

_____ 16. George Washington was known for being:

        a. a scientist
        b. an author
        c. a president
        d. a musician

_____ 17. Which would be considered a northern city?

        a. Mobile, Alabama
        b. Chicago, Illinois
        c. San Diego, California
        d. Orlando, Florida

_____ 18. A good student should use:

        a. an assignment notebook
        b. an umbrella
        c. black ink
        d. mustard and ketchup

_____ 19. The *divisor* in a division problem is:

        a. the answer
        b. the number being divided
        c. the number that's divided into another number
        d. the symbol for a division problem

Essay

Answer two of these three essay questions. Write at least one paragraph for each answer.

20. Explain the process you should follow to take a multiple-choice test.

21. What are other ways a teacher can find out how much a student has learned besides giving tests or quizzes? List and explain your ideas.

22. Why is a person's education important?

Practice for Testing

It's time to practice what you've learned. Choose some activities you can do to practice preparing for and taking tests. Use the list below to help you.

- [ ] Think of questions to ask your teacher about your next test so you know exactly what to expect. Then, ask the teacher your questions.

- [ ] Get study sheets or set up a review time with your teacher for your next quiz or test.

- [ ] Develop a study plan for your next test. Plan when, where, and what you'll study.

- [ ] Form a study group. Study together for your next test.

- [ ] Find out what kinds of questions will be on your next test. Then, review the tips for answering those types of questions before you take your test.

- [ ] Make up test questions as a way to study for your next test. Then, exchange your questions with someone else from the same class and see how you do.

Now, write down the activities you try in the chart below. Fill in the following information for each activity:

✔ Tell when you did the activity.

✔ Describe the activity.

✔ Explain how well you think the activity worked.

Date	Activity	How Well It Worked
April 3	Went to a review session for Biology.	Got a higher grade than usual!

Clinton D. Fentonbenton's Amazing Facts

Amazing Fact #1: The easiest test ever given was a spelling test made by Mr. John T. Bonecrunch. There was only one question on the test. The question was, "Spell your name." Eighteen out of the twenty students in Mr. Bonecrunch's 7th grade class received 100% on the test. The two students who failed this spelling test were twin brothers named Bill and Gill Filltiwill.

Amazing Fact #2: On the planet Oinkton, young porklets never take tests at school. But then, on the planet Oinkton, there are no schools.

Amazing Fact #3: The first math test was printed in 827 B.C. by Addicus Correctus. Addicus made one big mistake. He printed all the answers and asked his students to write down all the questions.

In this unit, you'll explore your attitude toward learning. You'll learn about internal and external behavior control and how YOU choose the way you behave.

You'll discover what motivates you to make your choices. You'll be asked to think about the choices you make in school and the rest of your life. And you'll explore your relationships with teachers and other adults.

This unit is different from the other units in this book. In the other units, you learned a skill. For example, you learned how to take notes, how to study for tests, or how to manage your time. But in this unit, you will not be trying to learn a specific skill.

The goal of this unit is to help you understand your responsibility for learning and for making good decisions. You will see that how well you do in school and life depends on two things:

✔ your attitudes and feelings about school and learning

✔ your willingness to take responsibility for your thoughts, feelings, and actions

Only YOU can decide how you think, feel, and act. (Phew! Enough philosophy for now!)

For a while there, I didn't have a very good attitude toward school. I thought it was everyone else's fault that I wasn't doing well.

One time my dad asked me, "How do you like school?" I said, "Closed!"

Who's in Control?

Hey, Mack! Come here. I have an assignment for you. I'm working on a special case, you see. I want you to complete *Clinton D. Fentonbenton's Who's in Control Rating Scale*. Okay? Okay.

My rating scale will tell you who you think controls your behavior — you or someone else. But listen, don't be a stooge. It would be a real crime if you put down answers that weren't true for you.

Circle A, B, C, or D for each statement below.

Clinton D. Fentonbenton's Who's in Control Rating Scale

almost always A	most of the time B	sometimes C	almost never D
1. I am responsible for my own behavior.			A B C D
2. I care about how I do in school.			A B C D
3. I believe that doing homework helps determine the grades I get.			A B C D
4. My mood depends on how others treat me.			A B C D
5. If something goes wrong, I blame other people for what happened.			A B C D

Circle the letter of the answer that best describes you.

6. If I get a good grade on an assignment, it's because:

    A   I worked for the grade

    B   someone helped me

    C   the assignment was easy

    D   I was lucky

7. If I get a poor grade on an assignment, it's usually because:

    A   I didn't try

    B   I was unlucky

    C   the assignment was too difficult

    D   no one would help me

Who's in Control?, *continued*

8. If I get a good grade on a test, it's because:
    A   I know the answers
    B   I was lucky
    C   the test was easy
    D   the teacher likes me

9. If I get a poor grade on a test, it's because:
    A   I didn't study the right things for the test
    B   I was unlucky
    C   the test was unfair
    D   the teacher dislikes me

10. If I need to do better in school:
    A   I should ask my teachers for help
    B   I should work harder
    C   tests and assignments should be easier
    D   teachers should tell me what to do

Find your total by using the guidelines below.

Give yourself 4 points for each A you circled.   _____   X 4 = _____

Give yourself 3 points for each B you circled.   _____   X 3 = _____

Give yourself 2 points for each C you circled.   _____   X 2 = _____

Give yourself 1 point for each D you circled.   _____   X 1 = _____

Total Points   = _____

Check the rating below that matches your total points.

☐ 10 – 20 points   I have an *external* sense of behavior control.   I think others control most of what happens to me.

☐ 21 – 30 points   I have a *mixed* sense of behavior control.   I think I control what happens to me some of the time.

☐ 31 – 40 points   I have an *internal* sense of behavior control.   I think I control what happens to me most of the time.

Your Learning Attitude

When you talk about attitudes, it's important to talk about behavior. *Behavior* is how you act or how you show your attitudes. Let me ask you a question. Who controls your behavior?

Many people believe that their behavior is controlled by other people or by situations. They say things like, "You made me mad" or "It wasn't my fault I got a speeding ticket." They think other people or other situations cause them to act the way they do.

When things go wrong, these people try to blame other people. But what's really weird is they blame other people when things go right, too. They say things like, "Oh well, I guess I just got lucky." If someone compliments them on their appearance, they might say, "My mom bought me this outfit."

People who often blame others for the way they act have an *external*, or outside, sense of behavior control. There are two kinds of behavior control — internal and external.

External Control

With *external control*, the feeling of behavior control comes from *outside* the person.

If you have an external sense of behavior control, you think *other people* or *other situations* control the way you act. You feel that other people or situations are responsible for what happens to you.

Internal Control

With *internal control,* the feeling of behavior control comes from *within*, or inside, the person.

If you have an internal sense of behavior control, you believe that *you* control the way you act. You feel responsible for your behavior.

People with an internal sense of behavior control might say things like, "If I think it through more the next time, maybe that won't happen," or "I know I can raise my grade if I study harder for my next test."

Being a responsible and dependable student means having *internal* behavior control. If you're responsible, YOU decide what happens to you in school. And YOU choose how you act in your classes.

Your Learning Attitude, *continued*

Review what you've just learned about internal and external control by answering these questions.

1. Behavior control can be _____ or _____ .

2. Jessica has an *external* sense of behavior control.   Jessica believes the control for her behavior
   is located _____ her.
                    (inside/outside)

   Jessica thinks _____ is responsible for her behavior.
                   (she/someone else)

3. Frank has an *internal* sense of behavior control.   Frank believes that control for his behavior
   is located _____ him.
                    (inside/outside)

   Frank thinks _____ is responsible for his behavior.
                (he/someone else)

4. True   False   A responsible student will most likely have an external sense of behavior control.

5. Suppose you just got a C on a test and you weren't pleased with your grade.   What would
   you say if you had an *external* sense of behavior control?

6. Imagine the boss at the fast-food restaurant where you applied for a job just called to say you
   were hired.   What would you say if you had an *internal* sense of behavior control?

7. Do you think you have an *internal* or *external* sense of behavior control?   How can you tell?

Internal or External?

Have you ever noticed that some people always have an excuse? When I, Clinton D. Fentonbenton, was in high school, I knew a girl named Dorthea Stewpot. She was always complaining about something. And no matter what went wrong, it was never her fault.

In fact, we called her "No-Fault" Stewpot. She was probably a nice enough person, but no one liked to be around her because she complained so much. And if anything did go wrong, she'd probably try to blame you.

Dorthea once kicked her little brother in the stomach. She said it was all his fault. He shouldn't have turned around. Whew! Now that's a person with an external sense of behavior control.

Test your knowledge of behavior control. Circle *Internal* or *External* for each of the following statements about behavior control.

1.	I feel nervous today.	Internal	External
2.	I didn't do my homework last night because I watched TV instead.	Internal	External
3.	You make me upset.	Internal	External
4.	I got an A on the test because it was easy.	Internal	External
5.	My baby sister kept me from finishing the assignment.	Internal	External
6.	I did great on the test because I studied.	Internal	External
7.	I'm always late for school because I shut off my alarm and go back to sleep.	Internal	External
8.	I didn't have any clothes to wear because my sister forgot to do the laundry.	Internal	External
9.	I can't get my homework done because my teachers give me too much.	Internal	External
10.	I'm taking extra baby-sitting jobs so I can buy a new outfit for the dance.	Internal	External

Discuss your answers with your classmates. Do you agree on the differences between internal and external sense of behavior control?

Choices, Choices

Every day of your life, you make hundreds of behavior choices. You choose what to eat, what to wear, what to read, and how to act.

You choose when to leave, who to talk to, which way to go, and what to listen to. Just think of it! You choose all of these behaviors (and more) every day.

Name three choices you made today. _____

_____

Most of the choices you make are not all that important. Some of the choices you make are very important. Everything you do, you choose to do.

Now we all make mistakes. Even I, Clinton D. Fentonbenton, make mistakes. Like once I tried to earn money by taking care of 400 rabbits in my backyard. Boy, was that a hare-raising experience!

When you make a mistake, it's because you choose the wrong thing to do. You need to make the right behavior choices as often as you can.

The student who is successful and has a good learning attitude does many things:

✔ He makes behavior choices that lead to success.

✔ He has an internal sense of behavior control.

✔ He shows responsible behavior.

1. Write your definition of what it means to be *responsible*.

   _____

2. Write the dictionary's definition of *responsible*.

   _____

3. How are the definitions different? How are they alike?

   _____

4. Give two examples of how you chose to be responsible this week.

   a. _____

   b. _____

Responsible Behavior

> **Being Responsible:** being in control of your behavior; thinking of the consequences before you act

Suppose you promised your dad you'd be home right after school to watch your little brother. A friend asks you to stop by his house on the way home from school to listen to a new tape. If you handle this situation responsibly, you:

A. stop by your friend's house for a little while and then go home

B. call your dad to ask if you can come home later

C. go directly home

If you answered B or C, you chose a "responsible" answer.

Read each situation below. Then, tell what you would do to handle each situation responsibly.

1. You arrive for your first period class five minutes late.

   _____

   _____

2. You just remembered that you have a four-page English report due tomorrow and you have been invited out for pizza and a movie tonight.

   _____

   _____

3. You volunteer to help work at a football concession stand, but you get sick and can't help.

   _____

   _____

4. You get home after play practice and can't remember your math homework assignment.

   _____

   _____

Motivation

Do you always know why you do the things you do?   I bet not.   We all do things, or are *motivated*, for different reasons.   What motivates me to do something may not motivate you at all.

For example, I am motivated to work extra hours to pay for Travel Agent School.   You might work extra hours so you can buy a special gift for a friend.

At the Ooey Gooey Ice Cream Factory, Doris Dimple loves to work extra hours.   She's a taste tester for all 47 flavors!

Are you motivated to be a good student?   This page and the next will help you understand why you are or are not motivated to be a successful student.

Answer these questions as honestly as you can.

1. Do you care about learning?   Why? _____

   _____

2. Do you feel good when you do well on a test?   Why? _____

   _____

3. Do you feel bad when you do poorly on a test?   Why? _____

   _____

4. Do you like to join clubs and belong to groups?   Why? _____

   _____

5. Do you enjoy being able to make your own decisions?   Why? _____

   _____

6. Do you enjoy being the center of attention?   Why? _____

   _____

Motivation, *continued*

7. Do you like to control people and situations?   Why?   _____

   _____

8. What parts of the school day do you enjoy?   Why?   _____

   _____

9. What parts of the school day are boring for you?   Why?   _____

   _____

10. What parts of the school day do you like the least?   Why?   _____

    _____

11. How do your parents try to motivate you?   Why?   _____

    _____

12. How do your teachers try to motivate you?   Why?   _____

    _____

13. How do your friends try to motivate you?   Why?   _____

    _____

14. What other things motivate you to do something?   Why?   _____

    _____

Based on your answers to these questions, do you think you're motivated to be a successful student?
Why?   If not, what might motivate you more?

_____

_____

Remember, YOU control what happens to you.   To be a successful student, YOU need to motivate
yourself.   Only YOU know what really matters to you.   And YOU need to make choices every day that
show you're responsible and want to succeed.

Attitude Survey

Your attitude toward your teachers can affect your grades and how you feel about learning. What is your attitude toward teachers?

Respond to the statements below to find out more about your attitude toward your teachers. Check the answer that best describes your feelings. Later, discuss your answers with the class.

	Disagree	No Opinion	Agree
1. Most teachers try to make learning difficult for students.			
2. Most teachers teach because they enjoy being around young people.			
3. If a student fails to learn, it is most likely the teacher's fault.			
4. Teachers should be able to tell when students need extra help.			
5. Most teachers are unwilling to help students with special learning problems.			

In a small group, discuss the following questions.

What effect does your attitude (positive or negative) toward teachers have on your learning?

Why can't a teacher make a student learn?

Teachers Are Human

Teachers are not out to make things difficult for students. On the other hand, teachers are not out to make things easy for students, either. Teachers believe that they can give a student the opportunity to learn, but they cannot make a student learn.

What does the paragraph above mean to you? _____

_____

There was a time when I, Clinton D. Fentonbenton, was unable to talk to my teachers. I knew I needed help with my schoolwork, but I wasn't able to talk to my teachers about it. Maybe I was afraid of them, I don't know.

I somehow thought that my school problems would just go away. They didn't. Not until I started talking to my 9th grade English teacher, Mr. Justin. I told you about him in the *Hello*, or introduction, to this book.

Anyway, I had to learn that being responsible for my own learning meant I needed to talk to my teachers. I also had to learn that I could do it. Let me tell you what I learned about teachers.

Teachers are human. They cry, they eat, they have families, they enjoy a good joke, they dream, and they even make mistakes. They are a lot like you and me.

Most teachers teach because they like young people — they like people like you and me. They also enjoy the feeling of being helpful.

What do you think are the characteristics of a good teacher? _____

_____

What do you think are the characteristics of a good student? _____

_____

Asking for Help

I learned that many demands are placed on a teacher's time. Most teachers are very willing to give extra time to help students improve their grades.

But most teachers want students to come to them and ask for help. A student who is willing to ask for help really wants the help.

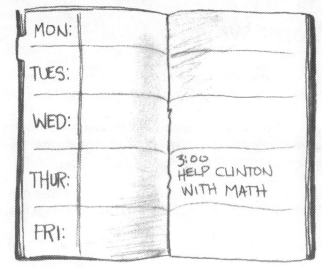

What to Do When You Ask for Help

1. *Make an appointment.* Make it private. Make it convenient for your teacher. It would not be cool on your part to say, "Gee, Mr. Toebone, I can't see you before school because I like to sleep as late as I can."

2. *Ask your teacher what you must do to get better grades.* With your teacher's help, come up with a plan, a routine, or a schedule. Be specific. Plan exactly what you need to do and when you need to do it.

3. *Follow your plan.* After a short while, check back with your teacher. Discuss how well the plan is working. Change your plan if you need to.

4. *Thank your teacher.* Remember, your teacher is doing extra work to help YOU solve YOUR problem. Just like you and me, teachers are more willing to help people who appreciate their efforts.

How would you handle this situation? You know you need help in math class. You want to ask your teacher for help. Write down exactly what you would say and do.

_____

_____

_____

Here are four ways to show your teachers you're trying to learn:

✔ Attend class every day.

✔ Show good listening skills in class.

✔ Ask questions.

✔ Hand in your assignments on time.

Don't Worry

You've learned that your attitude toward schoolwork and your teachers can affect how well you do in school.   But the things you worry about and how much you worry can affect your school success, too.

Some students worry about their schoolwork.   Some students worry about a boyfriend or girlfriend. Some students worry about their looks and what their friends think of them.   And some students worry without knowing why.

How much you worry and what you worry about can affect your success as a student.   The following activity will help you learn more about the things that worry you.

Think about each thing in the box below.   Then, list 10 things in order according to how much you worry about each thing.   Add other things to the list if you need to.

sports/gym class	library/cafeteria	using the chalkboard
homework	oral reports	parents/family
study hall	classmates	friends
teachers	asking a teacher for help	work
tests	answering in class	boyfriend/girlfriend
my looks		

Worry the Most

1. _____

2. _____

3. _____

4. _____

5. _____

6. _____

7. _____

8. _____

9. _____

10. _____

Worry the Least

For the two things you worry about most, decide what you might do to worry less about them.

1. _____

2. _____

Away with Stress

If you worry a lot, then you have stress.   If you feel like you are under pressure, then you have stress.

If you have a lot of stress, your ability to learn may suffer.   If you have stress, you may pay more attention to your worries than you do to school and other things.

A student who is overly stressed may not have a good attitude toward learning.   This is especially true if the source of stress is school-related.

When you have too much stress, you need to do something about it.   Here are some ways to reduce stress.   Choose those ways that will help you handle the things that worry you.

---

10 Ways to Reduce Stress

1. Balance your time between school, work, and play.
2. Eat right.
3. Get enough sleep.
4. Identify the cause of your stress.
5. Try to solve the problem that's causing the stress.
6. Ask for help from your friends, family, teachers, or other people you trust.
7. Think with your head as well as your heart.
8. Start a new hobby or other activity.
9. Do daily physical exercise.
10. Take short "mental vacations" during the day (during study halls, lunch breaks, or quiet times).

What are some other ways you can reduce stress?

_____

_____

In a small group, discuss the following questions.

1. How does stress affect learning?

2. What are *symptoms*, or signs, of stress?

3. Is stress ever a good thing?   Explain why.

4. How can you help a classmate who has too much stress?

Clinton D. Fentonbenton's **Amazing Facts**

Amazing Fact #1: On January 7, 1991, Margaret Earshot asked her chemistry teacher for help with her "gasoline" experiment that just wasn't working right.   The teacher said, "You had a bum wire."   Margaret thought he said, "You add some fire."   The chemistry lab can now be found on the baseball field near third base.

Amazing Fact #2: In 1962, Pauline Papercut chose to attend Crocklock High School.   Believe it or not, Pauline still goes to Crocklock every day.   She has to — she's the principal.

Amazing Fact #3: Recent studies indicate that most students become anxious during tests.   Wow! Saying that students get nervous when they take tests is about as obvious as saying the Atlantic Ocean has a lot of water!

Amazing Fact #4: A FINAL EXAM is not as terminal as it sounds!

How do you like to learn new things?   Do you like to read about them?   Do you like to watch a TV show about something new or listen to the radio?   Or do you like to learn about new things by actually doing them?

In this unit, you'll find out about learning styles.   You will see how you learn best.   Not everyone learns new things in the same way.   We learn in three main ways:

- ✔ visual — by seeing
- ✔ auditory — by hearing and listening
- ✔ tactile/kinesthetic — by touching or moving

How we learn depends on what feels right for us.   The way we learn also depends on how the information is presented to us.   For example, many of your teachers may expect you to learn by listening to lectures or class discussions.

But what can you do if you learn best by seeing things instead of listening?   You can learn to *adapt*, or change, your learning style to fit the situation you're in.   If you can do that in school, you're likely to be a successful student.

You know, a chameleon has to change or adapt all the time.   I had a pet chameleon once. His name was Larry.   But he didn't last long.   He had an identity crisis when I put him on a plaid tablecloth!

Learning Style

We all learn in different ways.   To get you thinking about your style of learning, I, Clinton Denton Fentonbenton, want to tell you about three of my friends.

Edward Eyebrow has a *visual* learning style.   He likes to learn by reading or by watching and observing things.

Ethel Earlobe has an *auditory* learning style.   She likes to learn by listening.

Henrietta Handy has a *tactile/kinesthetic* learning style.   She likes to learn by doing things.

Now, read each statement below.   Choose which of my friends the statement describes.

_____   1. I learned the words to my favorite song by playing it over and over on my tape player.

_____   2. I have to look at my fingers when I type.

_____   3. I forget a phone number unless I write it down.

_____   4. I can remember the story we read in English class better if my teacher or classmates read it aloud.

_____   5. My favorite class is chemistry because I like doing the experiments.

_____   6. I like reading an assignment better than having a class discussion.

Write your definition of *learning style* below.

_____

_____

Look It Up

Find these words in your dictionary. Write the definitions below.

Auditory _____

_____

Visual _____

_____

Tactile _____

_____

Kinesthetic _____

_____

This activity required you to read and write. First, you read the words on this page. Second, you read the definitions of the words in your dictionary. Third, you wrote the definitions on the lines above.

✔ When you were *reading*, you were using your *visual* learning style.

✔ When you were *writing*, you were using your *tactile* and *kinesthetic* learning styles.

Because the tactile learning style (by touch) is so similar to the kinesthetic learning style (by movement or muscle feeling), they are grouped together and called the *tactile/kinesthetic* learning style.

If someone had read the definitions above to you before you wrote them, what learning style would you have been using? Explain your answer.

_____

_____

_____

Learning by Example

The three main learning styles are visual, auditory, and tactile/kinesthetic.   With a partner, discuss the definitions of the learning styles you wrote on page 153.   Take turns quizzing each other.   Then, write an example of something a person might learn with each style.

Learning Style	Example
Visual	
Auditory	
Tactile/Kinesthetic	

This activity required you to listen, discuss, read, and write.

- ✔ When you were *listening* and *discussing* your examples, you were using your *auditory* learning style.

- ✔ When you were *reading*, you were using your *visual* learning style.

- ✔ When you were *writing*, you were using your *tactile/kinesthetic* learning style.

In the space below, draw pictures to help explain or remind you of each learning style.

Auditory	Visual	Tactile/Kinesthetic

Explain and discuss your pictures with a classmate or your teacher.

This activity required you to read, draw, and discuss.

- ✔ When you were *reading*, you were using your *visual* learning style.

- ✔ When you were *drawing*, you were using your *tactile/kinesthetic* learning style.

- ✔ When you were *discussing*, you were using your *auditory* learning style.

Visual Learning Style

Are you a visual learner?   Complete *The Official Clinton D. Fentonbenton Visual Learning Preference Scale* to find out.   Be honest.

There are no right answers to this preference scale.   There are only answers that are right for you.   This won't hurt a bit.

Circle A, B, or C for each statement below.

The Official Clinton D. Fentonbenton Visual Learning Preference Scale

very much like me A	sort of like me B	not like me C
1. I understand math problems better when they are written than when they are spoken.		A B C
2. I would rather read a story to myself than have one read to me.		A B C
3. I am interested in the colors, shapes, and sizes of things in my environment.		A B C
4. I understand written directions better than spoken directions.		A B C
5. It is easier for me to remember a telephone number I see than a telephone number I hear.		A B C
6. It is easier for me to remember a spelling word if I see it written than if someone spells it out loud.		A B C
7. It helps me to remember things if I close my eyes so I can "see" them in my head.		A B C
8. It is easy for me to memorize short poems or math facts if I can read them.		A B C
9. I prefer to take notes from the chalkboard than to take them while I'm listening.		A B C
10. When I read a textbook, the first things I look at are the pictures, charts, and graphs.		A B C

Visual Learning Style, *continued*

Find your total points by using the guidelines below.

Give yourself 3 points for each A you circled.   _____   X 3 = _____

Give yourself 2 points for each B you circled.   _____   X 2 = _____

Give yourself 1 point for each C you circled.   _____   X 1 = _____

Total Points = _____

Check the rating below that matches your total points.

☐ 24 – 30 points   I have a HIGH visual preference.

☐ 17 – 23 points   I have a MEDIUM visual preference.

☐ 10 – 16 points   I have a LOW visual preference.

Visual Preference

You have now taken *The Official Clinton D. Fentonbenton Visual Learning Preference Scale.* (If you haven't, then what are you waiting for? Do not pass Go. Do not collect $200. Go back two pages, finish the activity, then complete this page.)

Fill in the Blanks

I, _____, have completed *The Official Clinton D. Fentonbenton Visual Learning Preference Scale*.

My score was _____ points. This score indicates that I have a _____ visual preference.

✔ A *high preference* for visual learning means that you learn mostly by looking, watching, reading, and observing.

✔ A *medium preference* for visual learning means that you use your visual learning style, along with other learning styles.

✔ A *low preference* for visual learning may mean that you learn better using your other learning styles. Even if you have a low visual preference, you still learn some things by watching, reading, and observing.

Remember, we all learn in different ways. The key is to know how you learn best. You can also *adapt*, or change, the way you learn to fit the way your teacher teaches.

---

11 Ways to Be a Better Visual Learner

1. Occasionally change the color of ink in your pens.
2. Look at all the pictures, charts, and graphs in your textbooks.
3. Read all of your assignment directions.
4. *Visualize*, or see in your mind, new vocabulary or spelling words.
5. Read the class topic the day before it is discussed in class.
6. Visualize the details of what you read.
7. Examine the bulletin boards and other things on your classroom walls for connections to lessons.
8. Use a colorful highlighter to point out important information in your reading.
9. Visualize yourself doing what you are trying to learn.
10. Pay attention to the details of pictures.
11. Learn new things by seeing, observing, and reading.

Auditory Learning Style

Are you an auditory learner?   Here's your
chance to take *The Incredibly Awesome Clinton D.
Fentonbenton Auditory Learning Preference Scale.*

Because you're so cool, I'll let you take it free.
Be sure to choose only the answers that are right
for you.

Circle A, B, or C for each statement below.

The Incredibly Awesome Clinton D. Fentonbenton Auditory Learning Preference Scale

very much like me A	sort of like me B	not like me C
1. I understand a math problem better if I say the numbers to myself as I do the problem.		A B C
2. I would rather have a story read to me than to read it silently.		A B C
3. It is easier for me to remember things I hear than to remember things I read.		A B C
4. I learn more from class discussions than I do from reading in a textbook.		A B C
5. It is easy for me to sound out new words when I read.		A B C
6. It is easy for me to remember jokes or songs I hear.		A B C
7. I enjoy talking or singing.		A B C
8. It is easier for me to remember a telephone number I hear than a telephone number I see.		A B C
9. I understand spoken directions better than written directions.		A B C
10. When the teacher writes something on the chalkboard, it helps me to read it aloud.		A B C

Auditory Learning Style, *continued*

Find your total points by using the guidelines below.

Give yourself 3 points for each A you circled.   _____ X 3 = _____

Give yourself 2 points for each B you circled.   _____ X 2 = _____

Give yourself 1 point for each C you circled.   _____ X 1 = _____

                                               Total Points = _____

Check the rating below that matches your total points.

☐   24 – 30 points   I have a HIGH auditory preference.

☐   17 – 23 points   I have a MEDIUM auditory preference.

☐   10 – 16 points   I have a LOW auditory preference.

Auditory Preference

Well, what did you think of *The Incredibly Awesome Clinton D. Fentonbenton Auditory Learning Preference Scale*?   Do you have a high, medium, or low preference for auditory learning?

Fill in the Blanks

I, _____, have completed *The Incredibly Awesome Clinton D. Fentonbenton Auditory Learning Preference Scale.*

My score was _____ points.   This score indicates I have a _____ auditory preference.

- ✔ A *high preference* for auditory learning means that you learn mostly by listening and hearing.

- ✔ A *medium preference* for auditory learning means that you use your auditory learning style, along with other learning styles.

- ✔ A *low preference* for auditory learning may mean that you learn better through one of the other learning styles.   Even if you have a low auditory preference, you still learn some things by listening and hearing.

Remember, this is not a competition.   The trick here is to understand how you learn best.   When you know how you learn best, you can *adapt*, or change, the way you learn to the way your teacher teaches or to the way you need to study.   You'll learn more about that later.

---

13 Ways to Be a Better Auditory Learner

1. Make tapes of your class notes and then listen to them.
2. Tape record lectures and discussions in class.
3. Remember details by trying to "hear" previous discussions.
4. Say new vocabulary words and spelling words out loud.
5. Participate in class discussions.
6. Ask questions and volunteer answers in class.
7. Read your assignments out loud.
8. Read your assignments into a tape recorder.   Listen to the tape later.
9. After hearing about a topic, read about it.
10. Whisper new information to yourself.
11. Pay close attention to the changes in your teacher's voice (soft/loud).
12. Remember details by saying them over and over.
13. Pay close attention to spoken instructions.

Tactile/Kinesthetic Learning Style

Are you a tactile/kinesthetic learner?   Complete *The Supercharged Clinton D. Fentonbenton Tactile/Kinesthetic Learning Preference Scale* to find out.   It's fast.   It's powerful.   It's free.

It's important that you answer all questions honestly.   This test drive requires no helmet.

Circle A, B, or C for each statement below.

The Supercharged Clinton D. Fentonbenton Tactile/Kinesthetic Learning Preference Scale

very much like me A	sort of like me B	not like me C
1. I can remember a telephone number better when I write it down.		A B C
2. It helps me to learn if I can make or do a project that relates to my studies.		A B C
3. It helps if I touch my fingers to something as I add or count.		A B C
4. It's easier for me to learn new spelling words if I write them down.		A B C
5. I can remember a phone number better if I press the number buttons on the phone or if I dial the number.		A B C
6. I enjoy making things.		A B C
7. I can remember how to spell a word if I trace it with my finger.		A B C
8. I prefer to move around when I think.		A B C
9. Writing information down helps me to remember it.		A B C
10. I like to take things apart and put them back together.		A B C

Tactile/Kinesthetic Learning Style, *continued*

Find your total points by using the guidelines below.

Give yourself 3 points for each A you circled.   _____ X 3 = _____

Give yourself 2 points for each B you circled.   _____ X 2 = _____

Give yourself 1 point for each C you circled.   _____ X 1 = _____

                                   Total Points   = _____

Check the rating below that matches your total points.

☐   24 – 30 points   I have a HIGH tactile/kinesthetic preference.

☐   17 – 23 points   I have a MEDIUM tactile/kinesthetic preference.

☐   10 – 16 points   I have a LOW tactile/kinesthetic preference.

Tactile/Kinesthetic Preference

Did you like your test drive of *The Supercharged Clinton D. Fentonbenton Tactile/Kinesthetic Learning Preference Scale*?   I bet now you want one of your very own.   Talk with your teacher about that.   Did you show a low, medium, or high tactile/kinesthetic learning preference?

Fill in the Blanks

I, _____, have completed *The Supercharged Clinton D. Fentonbenton Tactile/Kinesthetic Learning Preference Scale*.

My score was _____ points.   This score indicates I have a _____ tactile/kinesthetic preference.

- ✔ A *high preference* for tactile/kinesthetic learning means that you learn mostly by doing things or making things.

- ✔ A *medium preference* for tactile/kinesthetic learning means that you use your tactile/kinesthetic learning style, along with other learning styles.

- ✔ A *low preference* for tactile/kinesthetic learning means that you learn better through one of the other learning styles.   Even if you have a low tactile/kinesthetic preference, you still learn some things by doing things or making things.

No matter what you scored on this activity, you can always get the checkered flag if you know how to study.   To win at school you must find out how you learn best, and try to adapt your style to the way your teachers teach.

---

10 Ways to Be a Better Tactile/Kinesthetic Learner

1. Learn by doing, touching, or practicing.
2. Write notes to yourself to help you remember things.
3. Take notes during lectures and discussions.
4. Type important information, like spelling words or notes.
5. Trace over new spelling words with your finger.
6. Take frequent "stand up and stretch" breaks.
7. Draw pictures of what you need to learn.
8. Move around quietly when you need to concentrate.
9. Build projects to help explain your ideas.
10. Frequently change pens and pencils so you have a different feel or grip as you write.

How You Learn

Here's a chart to help you review the three learning styles.   Below each learning style is an example of how a student might learn a specific skill with this learning style.

	Visual	Auditory	Tactile/Kinesthetic
Math Problems	needs to see them written	needs to hear them; says them to herself	needs to write them
Phone Number	needs to see it written	needs to hear it; repeats it to herself	needs to push buttons or dial it
Spelling Words	needs to read them	needs to hear them spelled out loud	needs to trace them with her finger
Directions	needs to see them written	needs to hear them read aloud	needs to write them

Knowing the learning style you prefer is very important.   Talk to your teacher about how you learn best.   Your teachers may let you try other ways to learn in their classes that fit your learning style better.

Here are some things you might suggest to your teacher.   After each suggestion is the learning style this activity matches.   Check the suggestions that might work for you.

☐ Bring a tape recorder to tape lectures and discussions. (auditory)

☐ Change your seat so you can hear or see better. (auditory/visual)

☐ Do a project instead of writing a paper. (tactile/kinesthetic)

☐ Listen to a story on tape or have someone read it out loud to you. (auditory)

☐ Spell words out loud to your teacher. (auditory)

☐ Act out a play instead of writing a paper. (tactile/kinesthetic)

☐ Do math problems on the chalkboard instead of on paper. (tactile/kinesthetic)

☐ Answer test questions orally instead of taking a written test. (auditory)

☐ Draw pictures, graphs, or charts of new information instead of writing a paper. (tactile/kinesthetic, visual)

How Teachers Teach

Another way to do better in class is to *adapt*, or change, your learning style to fit the way your teacher teaches.   For example, if your teacher usually talks or has class discussions, you'll need to use your auditory learning style.

Here are some ways teachers teach and the learning styles you need to use:

- ✔ lectures/class discussions (auditory)
- ✔ small group discussions (auditory)
- ✔ reading assignments (visual)
- ✔ films and videos (visual, auditory)
- ✔ overhead projector (visual, auditory)
- ✔ making a project (tactile/kinesthetic)
- ✔ role playing (auditory, tactile/kinesthetic)
- ✔ experiments (visual, tactile/kinesthetic)
- ✔ written assignments (visual, tactile/kinesthetic)

Refer to the lists on pages 157, 160, and 163 for ways to improve your visual, auditory, and tactile/kinesthetic learning styles.   If you can strengthen all your learning styles and adapt them to fit your teachers' teaching styles, you're on your way to being a top-notch student!

How do your teachers teach?   Fill in the chart below with your teachers' names and their teaching styles.   Refer to the list above for help.

Next, circle *A*, *V*, or *T/K* to show which learning style fits each teaching style best.   Then, use what you find out to help you learn better in each class!

Teacher	Teaching Style	Learning Style		
		A	V	T/K
		A	V	T/K
		A	V	T/K
		A	V	T/K
		A	V	T/K
		A	V	T/K
		A	V	T/K

A Style Quiz

For each statement below, match the learning style it best describes.   Write *A, V,* or *T/K* in front of each statement.

A = Auditory Learning Style   **V** = Visual Learning Style   **T/K** = Tactile/Kinesthetic Learning Style

_____ 1. Learns by listening

_____ 2. Remembers best if information is written down

_____ 3. Learns by watching

_____ 4. Remembers best when information is read aloud

_____ 5. Likes to build things

_____ 6. Remembers best when information is said

_____ 7. Can easily sound out unfamiliar words

_____ 8. Thinks best when moving around

_____ 9. Can easily see details in words

_____ 10. Learns by doing

_____ 11. Likes to read

_____ 12. Likes to sing

A Learning Tip

No matter which learning style you like best, constantly be on the lookout for new and different ways to learn.   This will make learning "the same old stuff" easier, and it will make learning more fun.

Learning with Style

Okay, so you know what kind of learning style you prefer.   Can you use your learning style to learn something new?

First, choose a topic from the list below or think of your own topic.

Next, decide what you'll do to learn more about the topic.   Read the list under your preferred learning style for ideas.

Then, complete your project and share it with the rest of your class.

<table>
<tr><td colspan="3" align="center">Topics</td></tr>
<tr><td colspan="3">

water pollution   oil painting
how a law is passed   how to score bowling
acting   making a newspaper
learning a new sport   using a computer
music or music trends   getting a job

</td></tr>
<tr>
<td>Visual

draw pictures, diagrams, or
   flow charts
make a bulletin board
write a report
watch someone paint, or act,
   or do a sport
read about the topic
see a videotape on the topic
</td>
<td>Auditory

give an oral report
hold a class discussion
have a debate
teach what you know to
   someone else
sing
recite poetry
listen to someone talk about
   the topic
interview someone about the
   topic
listen to tapes on the topic
</td>
<td>Tactile/Kinesthetic

act out a play
build something
create a game or sport
make a collage or mobile
make a poster, chart, or map
create a display or model
create or use a computer
   program
write and play a song
</td>
</tr>
</table>

Use the lines below to outline your ideas.

_____

_____

_____

_____

_____

Clinton D. Fentonbenton's Amazing Facts

Amazing Fact #1: When Megan Fullcloset first heard about learning styles, she thought it had to do with a mail order catalog featuring back-to-school fashions.

Amazing Fact #2: You've probably heard of 3-D vision. Well, in 1957, Audrey Tory invented 3-D hearing. It didn't work out too well. The red and blue cellophane kept getting stuck in her ears.

Amazing Fact #3: Jack Constructo is a tactile/kinesthetic learner. For American History class he made a statue of George Washington out of dog food and cement. He keeps it in his front yard. To this day, all the dogs in Jack's neighborhood wear dentures.

GOOD-BYE

I, Clinton D. Fentonbenton, don't need to tell you that school can be pretty tough sometimes. We all need help from time to time.

But even if you don't do as well in school as you'd like, that doesn't make you a bad person. Many great people have struck out in school at times, but have hit grand slams in the World Series of Life. Think about Einstein, for example!

Maybe you have trouble reading or doing math. Maybe you have trouble with reading *and* math. Or maybe you struggle with spelling.

Okay, so you work on improving those weak areas. You do your best to overcome those problems. But don't let your school problems become a LIFE problem. You must look inside yourself and see the good that is there. Then, share that good with everyone.

You can be a very kind, tender, generous, intelligent, and loving person even though you have difficulty reading. You can love and be loved even though you can't do long division.

My father, Kenton Fentonbenton, always said to me, "Clinton Fentonbenton, HOW you do in school is not as important as WHAT you do in school." My father is a very wise person.

I hope you found some ideas in this book that will help you get organized so you can do your best in school. I also wish you a very successful school career. It can make the difference of a lifetime!

Well, it's time to go. Thanks for letting me be your host for *Crash Course for Study Skills*.

It's been fun! Good-bye and Best of Luck!

Clinton D. Fentonbenton

Clinton D. Fentonbenton

Answer Key

Answers have been provided for questions with definite correct answers.   Judge the reasonableness of the responses for all other questions.

Unit 1:   Setting Goals

Answers will vary throughout this unit.

Unit 2:   Managing Time

pg. 37, It's About Time

1. 60
2. 30
3. 60
4. 24
5. 7
6. 52
7. 12
8. 10
9. clock, watch
10. calendar

pg. 45, Calendar Quiz

1. January
2. February
3. March
4. April
5. May
6. June
7. July
8. August
9. September
10. October
11. November
12. December

1. - 8. Holidays will vary.

Pg. 50, Good Ideas Quiz

1. weekly
2. plan
3. calendar
4. monthly
5. study
6. every day
7. appointments
8. assignments
9. prioritize
10. great

Unit 3:   Listening

pg. 56, Concentration

concentrate — to direct your attention to one thing

move to the front of the room
tell herself to pay attention
block out outside noises
clear her desk

pg. 68, Fact or Feeling?

2. Facts: Electric Earthworms, concert, City Arena, Saturday, free ticket, gets to go, radio station
   Feelings: happy, excited

3. Facts: American History report, worked three hours, last night, looked great, left on bus, this morning
   Feelings: happy, pleased, frustrated, angry

4. Facts: 10 extra work hours this week, money for speakers, work Saturday and Sunday, can't go to movies
   Feelings: happy, excited, sad, disappointed

pg. 70, Paraphrasing

You sure spent a lot of time yesterday figuring out how to do your banking on your computer.

pg. 71, Paraphrasing Practice

b

Last summer you visited your cousins near Los Angeles for two weeks.

You need to review Chapters 5-7 and the handouts for Friday's test.   There are no essay questions and the test is worth 40 points.

U.S. government agencies now use girls' and boys' names to name powerful storms.

pg. 73, Listening Quiz

1. concentrate
2. feelings
3. question
4. ready
5. paraphrase
6. signals
7. verbal
8. show
9. argue
10. directions

Unit 4:   Taking Notes

pg. 80, The 5Ws & H

Who — eagles
What —Eagles are timid hunters who feed on fish and dead animals.   They are afraid of humans.
Where — North America
Why — Eagles symbolize freedom and power.
How — Eagles look fierce and proud.

pg. 86, **Prepare to Paint**

How to Paint a House

Have you ever helped someone paint a house?   <u>House painting takes place in two main steps.</u>

<u>The first step in house painting is called preparation.</u>   The painter makes sure that all of the (supplies and equipment are at the house to be painted.)   The (painter must scrape off all the loose and peeling paint) from the house.   After the scraping is done, (the painter must wash the house) to remove as much of the dirt as possible.

<u>The second step is the actual painting.</u>   Sometimes (a *primer*, or first coat, of paint is applied) before the finishing coat.   The painter usually (paints from the top of the house down to the bottom.) (Big areas are painted first.) (The trim is usually painted last.) (Neatness counts) on this job.

A. First step is preparation.
3. Wash the house.
4. Paint trim last.

pg. 87, **Painting Notes**

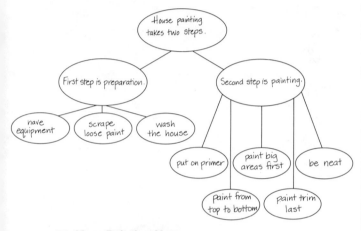

pg. 88, **More Painting Notes**

4. Scrape loose paint.
8. Paint from top to bottom.
10. Paint trim last.

pg. 91, **Quiz Time!**

1. Note taking helps you remember important information for class and for tests.
2. w/o   +
    etc.   e.g.
    w/   re:
3. c
4. b
5. Signal words will vary.
6. Who, what, where, when, why, and how — words that help you know the kind of information you should listen for or look for.

    Use the 5Ws & H when you are taking notes in class or when you are doing a reading assignment.

Unit 5:   Studying

pg. 111, **Grandma's Rule**

1. clutter
2. assignment
3. early
4. interruptions
5. out-of-chair body break

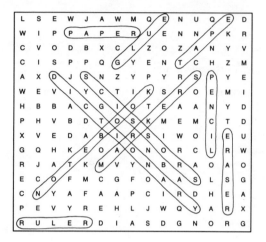

Unit 6:   Taking Tests

pg. 123, **Fill in the Blank**

1. vision
2. sense
3. iris
4. color, shape
5. inherited, color blindness
6. ophthalmologist
7. two, vision

pg. 124, **True or False?**

1. False
2. True
3. True
4. True
5. True
6. False
7. False
8. False
9. False

pg. 125-6, **Multiple Choice**

1. b
2. d
3. c
4. b
5. d
6. d
7. d
8. d

pg. 127, Matching Questions

1. c
2. a
3. b
4. f
5. g
6. h
7. k
8. a
9. b
10. i
11. a
12. d
13. c

pgs. 131-2, Testing Practice

1. horseshoes
2. rings
3. extinct
4. microscope
5. False
6. True
7. True
8. True
9. False
10. False
11. e
12. c
13. a
14. f
15. b
16. c
17. b
18. a
19. c
20. - 22. Answers will vary.

Unit 7:   Learning Attitude

pg. 139, Your Learning Attitude

1. internal, external
2. outside, someone else
3. inside, he
4. False
5. - 7. Answers will vary.

pg. 140, Internal or External?

1. Internal
2. Internal
3. External
4. External
5. External
6. Internal
7. Internal
8. External
9. External
10. Internal

Unit 8:   Learning Style

pg. 152, Learning Style

1. Ethel Earlobe
2. Edward Eyebrow
3. Henrietta Handy
4. Ethel Earlobe
5. Henrietta Handy
6. Edward Eyebrow

Learning Style — Definitions will vary.

pg. 153, Look It Up

Auditory — experienced through hearing
Visual — experienced through seeing
Tactile — experienced through touch
Kinesthetic — experienced through movement

Auditory, because you listened to someone read the definitions to you.

pg. 166, A Style Quiz

1. A
2. T/K
3. V
4. A
5. T/K
6. A
7. A or V
8. T/K
9. V
10. T/K
11. V
12. A

1-00-13